BOARD GAMES IN 100 MOVES

IAN LIVINGSTONE
AND JAMES WALLIS

Contents

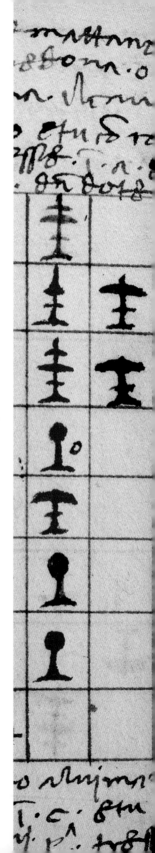

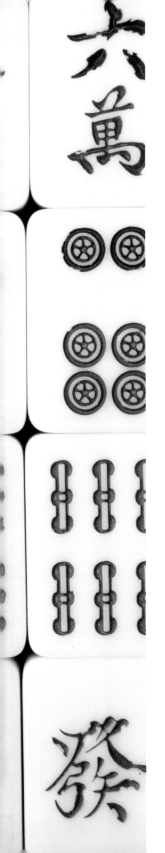

Foreword by Ian Livingstone

Game design has come a long way since pointless rules such as "roll six to start." I've been playing board games for as long as I can remember, and always will. Play is natural. We learn through play. And of course, it is fun. George Bernard Shaw once said, "We don't stop playing because we grow old; we grow old because we stop playing."

I learned to play Chess at an early age—card games, too—but got hooked on thematic board games in the early 1960s with Monopoly. I played it a lot! If I was winning a game, I wouldn't bother to collect the money owed to me by players who landed on Old Kent Road or Whitechapel Road, dismissing the low rents as "chicken feed." This gamesmanship earned me the nickname of "Feed," which stuck with me until the day I left school. While Monopoly does not feature high on my play list these days, I recently bought a 1955 edition in near-mint condition on eBay. It was nostalgia overload when I opened the box.

There is so much more choice these days. The annual SPIEL convention in Essen attracts tens of thousands of people looking for new games. A record number of 190,000 people attended in 2018 where some 1,800 new titles were released. And the internet has given board games a new lease on life thanks to specialty websites like BoardGameGeek, eBay, YouTube, and crowdfunding platforms such as Kickstarter.

Tabletop games are booming again, ironically in the age of video games. I discovered war games in the late 1960s, playing Diplomacy and Avalon Hill games such as Stalingrad. Play-by-mail games of Diplomacy would take months to play, but that was part of the allure—waiting for a letter or a phone call proposing an alliance. I used to help Don Turnbull publish his play-by-mail fanzine, *Albion,* occasionally illustrating the cover.

When he stopped publishing *Albion* in 1975, Don gave me his mailing list. Steve Jackson, John Peake, and I had just founded Games Workshop in our apartment in Shepherd's Bush, and we sent a copy of our new fanzine *Owl & Weasel* to Don's subscribers in an attempt to build a community of board game players. Gary Gygax, the cocreator of Dungeons & Dragons (D&D), read it and sent us a copy of D&D. We quickly became obsessed with D&D and pivoted our fledgling game company from traditional games to role-playing games. The year 1975 was when my hobby turned into a lifelong career.

I set up the Games Night Club in 1986, and we are still playing regularly, some 500 newsletters later. Strategy-based "Eurogames" are our preferred choice: modern classics such as Catan, Carcassonne, and Ticket to Ride. I never tire of trying out new games and have more than 1,000 in my collection. "What's your favorite game?" is a question I'm often asked. It's impossible to answer, but there are 100 of my favorites in this book, not necessarily the best 100 games of all time, but certainly game changers in their own right.

People also ask, "What makes a good game?" For me, it has to be easy to learn but difficult to master. Luck should play a minor role. A good game should offer lots of player choice, interaction, negotiation, and deal-making and deal-breaking opportunities. There should always be things to think about even when it's not your turn, so you don't get bored waiting. Aesthetically, it should have an exciting theme, lots of bits, and great artwork. Above all, it has to have clever game-play mechanics and a sprinkle of magic fairy dust that makes you want to come back and play it again. And again.

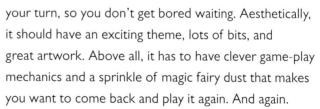

Ian Livingstone
Pictured, left, with some of his board game collection in 2018.

Introduction

We all play games. It is part of what makes us human. Other species play, but we Homo sapiens are the only ones that give ourselves rules and constraints to define what we can and can't do—and how we win.

Whether it's big, cardboard boxes full of counters and cards or armies of toy soldiers, silly social games around a table or little games we play to test ourselves, some in the real world and others in our heads, the desire to play games is hardwired into us. As children, games give us a safe way to understand and experiment with what is possible, permissible, and acceptable, to test ourselves and the limits of our world. As adults, they are an escape from everyday life, a way to spend time with friends—or make new ones—in an atmosphere of friendly competition and interesting challenges. And they are, above all else, fun.

Fun is, in fact, fundamental to what makes games attractive. That doesn't mean that games can't take on extra levels of meaning. From the way that the ancient Egyptians used Senet to describe and understand the soul's journey through the afterlife; to the medieval game Rithmomachia, created as a way of demonstrating the ideas of Boethian mathematics; to war games, business games, and educational games, this way of learning by doing is incredibly effective and has been practiced for thousands of years. Whether you realized it or not when you played it, Monopoly has been teaching children about investments, mortgages, taxation, and the perils of debt for generations. Not everything we learn from games is practical real-world information, but we absorb tactics and strategies, we understand the way the systems work, and we learn how to manipulate them—and how to manipulate our fellow players, too.

The heart of a game is a battle of wits, and the most interesting and least predictable opponent is another human being. Throughout history, almost all games have been for two or more players, pitted against each

other. Solo games were a rarity until computer gaming became a phenomenon in the 1980s, and even those have quickly gone back to multiplayer formats, as soon as processor power and the internet made it possible. Cooperative board games, where all the players work together to beat the system, arrived around the same time as computer games and have exploded in popularity in the last decade. The 21st century has seen new peaks of creativity among game designers, with new formats, ideas, and even technology giving birth to unprecedented numbers of new tabletop games.

In this book, we will show how closely games and culture are interwoven, how changes in technology and society have shaped games, and how games themselves have affected the development of human culture. It's possible to categorize games in hundreds of different ways: by the pieces they use, the style of play (race games, war games, trading games, for example), or the mechanics used to play them. But when you're talking about the history of games, one thing defines them more than any other: the materials they were made of.

The ages of games—at least the games we know about, the ones that have survived from ancient history—break down into the chapters you will find in this book: wood and stone, paper and print, cardboard, plastic, the imaginative influence of science fiction and fantasy, and, finally, the futuristic fusion of digital and physical. What will the next move be? We look forward to finding out.

"*VENARI LAVARI; LUDERE RIDERE; OCCEST VIVERE*" [To hunt; to bathe; to game; to laugh; this is to live]

INSCRIPTION ON A *LUDUS DUODECIM SCRIPTA* BOARD FOUND AT TIMGAD, ALGERIA, AROUND 100CE

Board Games in 100 Moves

It would be impossible to list and describe all the games in the world, so here
are the most groundbreaking, the most influential, the most successful,
and the ones that most reflect the times when they were at their peak.
This is the history of games boiled down to its 100 key examples.

1 Senet | 3100BCE
Played across Egypt for 3,000 years,
more than 80 sets of Senet have
been excavated, but reinventions
of the rules fail to capture what
made the pharaohs enjoy it so much.

2 Royal Game of Ur | 2600BCE
Probably evolved from Senet, this
fast race game spread across the
Middle East and into India 4,000
years ago and is still played today.

3 Hounds and Jackals | 2000BCE
"The game of 58 holes" is a
two-player race game with gambling
elements. Attempts to reconstruct
the lost rules lack excitement.

4 Mancala | 1000BCE
The great game of Africa, with
hundreds of variants and different
from other early games. This game
of skill should be played quickly.

5 Nine Men's Morris | Roman
The original match-three game,
Nine Men's Morris was spread
around Europe and beyond by the
Romans. Its boards were graffitied
around the world. Fast and fun.

6 Go | 400BCE
A game that looks simple but has
extraordinary depth and richness.
Probably the finest game of the ancient
world, and the finest game ever.

7 Hnefetafl | 400CE
Known as "the Viking game," there
are many different forms of Tafl
games, and today's rules may not be
the same. Demands careful tactics.

8 Backgammon | 500CE
The roll-and-move race game at
its most refined, balancing strategy
and luck in equal measure.

9 Chess | 600CE
Instantly recognizable and played
all over the world, Chess can be
dry and formal, but it's a game
every player ought to know.

10 • Rithmomachia | 1030

By mathematician monk Asilo of Würzburg, Rithmomachia is important but complicated to play. It's the forerunner of many trends and themes of modern games.

11 • Checkers | 1100

Often dismissed as a childish step on the way to Chess, Checkers is actually a tight, strategic game.

12 • Dominoes | 1150

The first and most famous tile-placing game, the history of Dominoes is obscure, but its cultural reach is huge.

13 • Playing cards | 1365

Card games you should know: Poker, Rummy, Blackjack (or Twenty-One), Cribbage, Solitaire, Whist, Bridge, Hearts, Idiot, Boodle, Euchre, Nertz (or Pounce), Go Fish, War, and Slapjack!

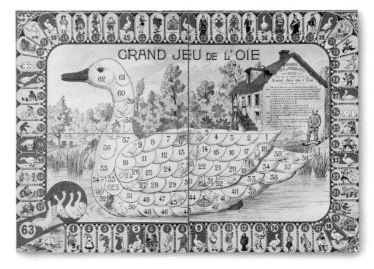

14 • Royal Game of the Goose | 1480

This lackluster game became the direct ancestor of the entire modern game industry. Pretty boards; shame about the gameplay.

15 • Pachisi | 1500s

Forget Ludo or Parcheesi, find the real rules for Pachisi on the internet, gather three friends, and play the game as it was originally intended.

16 • A Journey Through Europe | 1759

A reskin of the Royal Game of the Goose, this is one of the first educational games, and marks the point where games were published for children more than adults.

17 • Kriegsspiel | 1812

Impossible to play in its original form, the history of games would be very different without the existence of this dry and complex Prussian war game.

18 • Traveler's Tour Through the United States | 1822

The first game published in the US, by F. & R. Lockwood. It's historically important, but in play it's very similar to A Journey Through Europe.

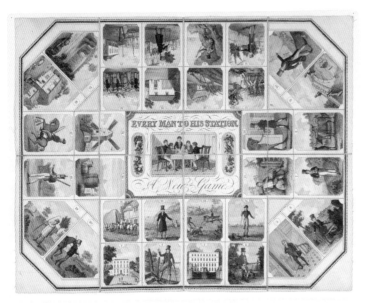

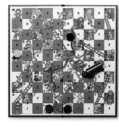

24

Snakes and Ladders | 1890s
Known as Chutes and Ladders in the US (1943), this game is purely random with no tactics, but it's the first game that many people ever play, and it's survived this long for a reason.

19

Every Man to His Station | 1825
Possibly the peak of the new wave of English games in the early 19th century, a beautifully illustrated engraved board with a worthy, if chauvinistic, educational message. Attractive artwork, but not exciting to play.

25

Pit | 1904
High entertainment at high volume, with lying and a lot of luck, Pit may be the most accurate simulation of stock-market trading ever released.

20

Liar's Dice | c.1800s
A great, fast mix of tactical play, dice rolling, push-your-luck optimism and lying to people's faces—that also reveals a lot about people. Can be played with poker dice.

22

Halma/Chinese Chequers | c.1880
The same game on different-shaped boards, this feels as well worn as a traditional game but is comparatively new. Worth playing to understand games, but very simple.

26

The Landlord's Game | 1903
The mother of Monopoly is amongst the first modern board games and provided the template for much 20th-century game design.

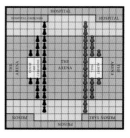

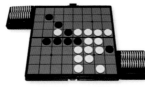

23

Reversi/Othello | c.1885
This clever counter-flipping game is also a great primer in strategy, teaching you to look for non-obvious moves and to think several moves ahead.

21

Mahjong | c.1850
The Chinese game of set building evolved from card games, but the tiles give it a tactile, ritual element that adds to the rich experience.

27

Suffragetto | 1909
This game may be dated, but the game play remains entertaining and it still deserves a vote of confidence. Physical boards are scarce, so you'll have to make your own version.

28 • Battleship | 1931
This game may be low on tactics
and high on lucky guesses,
but for simplicity and tension
it's still a direct hit.

29 • Monopoly | 1935
Popular but with a reputation for
being never-ending, Monopoly can
still offer a fast, cutthroat evening of
entertainment if you play by the
proper rules.

30 • Buccaneer | 1938
The classic game of piratical action,
Geoffrey Bull's Buccaneer is mostly
remembered for its wonderful
assortment of parts.

31 • Scrabble | 1938
Alfred Mosher Butts's definitive word
game, Scrabble comes to life when
you realize the best placements
score the most points.

32 • Subbuteo | 1946
Successful tabletop game Subbuteo's
flick-to-kick action of finger-shunting
plastic players on hemispherical bases
across a green baize pitch enthralled
generations of players.

33 • Clue/Cluedo | 1949
Anthony E. Pratt's Clue/Cluedo captures
the atmosphere of a country-house
murder mystery. Works well with
players of different ages and abilities.

34 • Candy Land | 1949
Eleanor Abbott's Candy Land is to
the US what Snakes and Ladders is
to the UK: the first game many
remember playing. Colored cards
or spinners are used instead of
dice, and players are sent
backward less often.

35 • Tactics | 1954
The first modern board-based war
game, Charles S. Roberts's Tactics
introduced a lot of ideas that are
standard today. War games have
advanced a lot since.

36 • Mille Bornes | 1954
The French game of road rallying ("a
thousand milestones") by Edmond
Dujardin is a fast-playing race card
game with obstacles such as red
lights, speed limits, and flat tires.

37 • Yahtzee | 1956
Edwin S. Lowe's Yahtzee is based
on several classic dice games.
It's the forerunner of the modern
roll-and-write genre of games.

38 • Diplomacy | 1959
Hugely influential and much imitated,
this classic game of strategy and
negotiation is still very playable.

11

43

Strat-O-Matic Baseball | 1963
The first successful sports simulation game, Strat-O-Matic Baseball is not so much a pastime as a cult in America and led to fantasy football.

39

Risk | 1959
The mirror-twin of Diplomacy, Risk's struggle for world supremacy has more random factors and is less likely to end in argument.

47

Mastermind | 1970
Preceded by the pencil-and-paper code-breaking game, Bulls & Cows, this two-player coloured peg puzzler by Mordecai Meirowitz was many children's introduction to logical deduction.

44

Mouse Trap | 1963
Mouse Trap's delightful contraption has excited generations of kids. Modern editions have redesigned the machinery.

48

Uno | 1971
The classic get-rid-of-your-cards game, Merle Robbins's fast and furious family classic is based on the traditional card game Crazy Eights.

49

Boggle | 1972
Scrabble's feisty dice-based nephew, Boggle gives players three minutes to find as many unique words as possible in a 4x4 grid of letters. Fast and competitive.

40

The Game of Life | 1960
Reuben Klamer and Bill Markham's revamp of the 1860 The Checkered Game of Life is a worthy successor. Decision-making keeps it interesting.

50

The Warlord | 1972
Think Risk with stronger tactics, strategic empire building, and nuclear brinkmanship; this is a tense battle for world domination with a clever bluffing combat mechanic.

41

Summit | 1961
A simulation of the Cold War, Summit puts each player in control of their country's economy and military. Taut and fraught, it's one of the progenitors of the field of political war games.

45

Acquire | 1964
Sid Sackson's classic of shares and takeovers has been described as the first Eurogame. Its simple, intelligent game play is still gripping today.

42

Formula 1 | 1962
Motor racing gave race games a boost in popularity, and Formula 1 captured the excitement of a Grand Prix with simple but clever mechanics and set the pace for the games that followed.

46

Nuclear War | 1965
Doug Malewicki's card game is steeped in dark humor. Can you be the last nation with any survivors? The mechanics are clever, and a "final retaliation" can mean that everyone loses.

51

Hare and Tortoise | 1973
David Parlett's diceless race game is not just a clever piece of game design; it's a challenging, entertaining, and thoroughly competitive brainteaser.

52 Connect 4 | 1974

Drop pieces into the grid to make a line of four. This much imitated modern classic can get strategic with the right players.

53 1829 | 1974

This is a train game for the cognoscenti, a brilliant mix of railroad running and share trading. Set aside an afternoon to play.

54 Crude | 1974

A Eurogame before they existed, Crude is about drilling, pumping, refining, and selling oil. It is now recognized for the early classic it is.

55 Dungeons & Dragons | 1975

A milestone in gaming history that genuinely changed the hobby. Ideas from D&D underpin a huge amount of modern game design—physical and digital.

56 Cosmic Encounter | 1977

The first exceptions-based game, where each player has a different special power that changes the way the game works. Cosmic Encounter remains a fun, brainteasing strategic challenge.

57 Civilization | 1980

Francis Tresham's game of building classic cultures of the Mediterranean, Civilization introduced innovative ideas like the tech tree and inspired the computer game of the same name. Takes eight hours to play properly, but worth it.

58 Can't Stop | 1980

A combination of push-your-luck and tactical decision-making. Sadly, Can't Stop's distinctive eight-sided board isn't seen much these days.

59 Trivial Pursuit | 1981

A general-knowledge quiz disguised as a board game, Trivial Pursuit laid the path for many to follow and is one of the games that defined the 1980s.

60 Sherlock Holmes Consulting Detective | 1981

Try to solve cases faster than the great detective in this evocative story-based game. Its mix of narrative and game play was 20 years ahead of its time.

61

Dark Tower | 1981
One of the first physical/digital games, Dark Tower is a board game with a digital tower at the center. Working copies are scarce.

62

The Warlock of Firetop Mountain | 1982
The hugely popular *Fighting Fantasy* series of single-player game books combined branching narrative with a simple dice-based role-playing system. Still in print today.

63

Jenga | 1982
What goes up must come down, but what's delightful about Leslie Scott's Jenga is how far up it's possible to go before a collapse.

64

Warhammer | 1983
The foundation of the modern Games Workshop empire, Warhammer's detailed rules for playing fantasy battles with armies of miniature figures have stood the test of time.

65

Heimlich & Co. | 1984
Also known as Top Secret Spies, this game of jockeying for position is great fun. It also introduced many ideas that are now standard, such as meeples.

66

Pictionary | 1985
The guess-the-drawing game is inspired equally by Trivial Pursuit and Charades, and sold 20 million copies by the end of the 20th century.

67

Blood Bowl | 1986
Games Workshop's game of ultraviolent American football in a fantasy world developed fast and has inspired comics and novels, as well as many other fantasy sports games.

68

Werewolf/Mafia | 1986
Invented in Russia, Mafia is the party game that created the bluffing/social-deduction/hidden-identity genre. Identify the mafia (or werewolves) before the werewolves (or mafia) kill everyone one by one. Paranoia has never been such fun.

69

Survive! | 1986
Help your tribe escape the crumbling island and get to safety using boats or dolphins, while avoiding sea monsters and sharks. The rules let players guide the threats onto each other's hapless pieces.

70 **HeroQuest | 1989**
Four archetypal adventurers explore a dungeon and fight monsters for treasure. Simple in plot but strategic in play, this was the template for a generation of dungeon-bashing board games.

71 **Modern Art | 1992**
A clever game of collecting paintings, you also have to auction part of your collection to earn money. Not just a game but a satire on the contemporary art scene.

72 **Magic: The Gathering | 1993**
Richard Garfield's Magic was the first collectible card game, created the genre, and made hundreds of millions of dollars. Now there's even a pro tour.

73 **Once Upon a Time | 1993**
The game that blends storytelling and game play to hilarious effect, Once Upon a Time weaves a single story from the cards in every player's hand. There can be only one ending and one winner, and that means many attempts to interrupt the storyteller.

74 **Dragon Dice | 1995**
TSR Hobbies's last big hit, this game of collectible dice with custom symbols on each side was a huge success. Its elegance and charm survive.

75 **Settlers of Catan | 1995**
Klaus Teuber's gentle settlements game is an unlikely one to have shaken the world but is the greatest Eurogame of its generation.

76 **El Grande | 1996**
Probably the least family-friendly game to win the Spiel des Jahres, El Grande is a masterpiece of tight, intelligent Eurogame design. Possibly Wolfgang Kramer's finest game.

77 **Apples to Apples | 1999**
A deceptively simple party game with humor and charm, Apples to Apples was a smash hit on launch. Its core mechanic has inspired other games, including Cards Against Humanity.

78 **Lost Cities | 1999**
Lay sequences of cards to mount archaeological expeditions to locate lost cities in this two-player game. Reiner Knizia later expanded his idea, but Lost Cities has a lovely simplicity to it.

79 **Carcassonne | 2000**
Everyone builds a map of a medieval city and its surrounding landscape by adding a tile on their turn. Klaus-Jürgen Wrede's Carcassonne is a true modern classic.

80 **The Princes of Florence | 2000**
Kramer's third game on this list, rich merchant princes try to outspend each other as patrons of the arts. Superb.

81 Puerto Rico | 2002
A piece of tight, elegant design, Andreas Seyfarth's Puerto Rico casts players as colonial governors. Gather victory points via transporting goods or making town improvements.

82 Ticket to Ride | 2004
Alan R. Moon's easily grasped game of completing train routes has huge appeal, and building up your network is a satisfying experience.

83 Power Grid | 2004
Build power stations and networks across Germany or the US, supplying cities with electricity. Intensely playable and rewarding to replay; by Friedmann Friese.

84 Memoir '44 | 2004
Richard Borg's two-player card-driven war game is based around D-Day. Win by gaining Victory Medals, not just by defeating your opponent.

85 Twilight Struggle | 2005
A memorable two-player re-creation of the Cold War, Twilight Struggle uses cards to re-create historical events, but not in the order you may remember and not with the same effects.

86 Caylus | 2005
An early and influential worker-placement game by William Attia, Caylus pits you as a master builder constructing a castle for the king of France. Agonizing decisions; deceptively complex.

87 Through the Ages | 2006
An old theme given a new twist. Vlaada Chvátil's Through the Ages has no map but creates a wonderful sense of managing a complex and evolving society across history.

88 Agricola | 2007
A heavyweight of modern Euro design, Uwe Rosenberg's Agricola challenges you to build and run a simple medieval farm. Hard but rewarding and well designed.

89 Pandemic | 2008
The cooperative-gaming masterpiece that launched a thousand imitators, in Matt Leacock's tense creation, players work together to save the world from disease.

90 Dixit | 2008
Dixit is based around a deck of cards with beautiful surreal images. Can you describe one so that some but not all the players can guess which one you're talking about? Dixit is about bluffing and verbal gymnastics, but also the pleasure of being a bit silly.

91

Dominion | 2008

Start with a small deck of cards and make it larger each round. Each new card has implications. A simple and brilliant idea by Donald X. Vaccarino.

97

Small World | 2009

Philippe Keyaerts's game is set on a fantasy world where there isn't enough room for everyone. Often tense and funny, it's a splendid twist on conquering a planet.

93

7 Wonders | 2010

From Antoine Bauza, this is one of the fastest games of building an empire. Simple structure but complex and very satisfying in play.

94

Machi Koro | 2012

A clever and simple city-building card and dice game from Masao Suganuma in Japan. Gentle and delightful; charming graphics.

95

Splendor | 2014

Easy to learn, this fast-moving and elegant engine-building race game generates plenty of choice and tension. Both art and components are superb and include very tactile poker-chip-style counters.

96

Codenames | 2015

An international hit from the Czech Republic, Codenames combines the cleverness of a modern Eurogame and the simplicity and fun of a party game in a surprisingly small box.

97

Exploding Kittens | 2016

A fairly simple push-your-luck card game, Exploding Kittens demonstrated how new platforms could connect designers and gamers.

98

Beasts of Balance | 2016

Beasts of Balance's stacking play is family friendly with gorgeous chunky pieces and clever emergent strategies. A physical/digital game hybrid.

99

Sushi Go Party! | 2016

The expanded version of the original Sushi Go, this fast and delightful game is easy to learn. It's a great modern family or party game and can keep serious gamers happy, too.

100

The Mind | 2018

So simple that some people insist it isn't really a game, The Mind is half guessing game, half mind-reading exercise and so simple that if you can count to 100, you can play. Will it be the start of the next big thing in games? Only time will tell.

WOOD AND STONE

The earliest games were made of wood and stone and played anywhere—using sticks to scratch marks in the dirt. Their rules had to be remembered and taught in person because not enough people could read and write, or because writing didn't exist yet.

Right: Folio from the Iranian *Shahnama* (Book of Kings) depicting wise man Buzurjmihr mastering the "Hindu Game of Chess," dated to 1530–1535. ***Above:*** Senet and Pachisi playing pieces.

همین رای و اندیشه بشیاری
همه کوش واریدگفتار اوی
جب و رایت صف بر کشیده سپاه
تقلب اندرون پناخته جانش
پارایت وانات یکی رمگاه
مبارز که اسب افکند بر دو زوی
بزم اندر و نش نماینده یا
شیشوار دبشتور برد و بشت شا
مدیت جب و رایت پرخنجوی
نمان پیل پنچکی ز بالای جای
وز و بر تراییان چکی بپای
همه انجمن در شکفتی باند
بماناندازان مردم پدار تخت
نفی شد و فرستاده بشنخت
جوبوز زرجهر آن سپه برالند

Who Goes First?

What's the oldest game you know?

Chess is a pretty good guess. It's 1,400 years old, maybe a little more, but in game terms, that makes it a teenager. Backgammon has it beaten by a couple of centuries, dating back to 400CE. Nine Men's Morris goes back even further: its origins are obscure, but the Romans definitely played it and transported it across their empire and beyond, making it at least two millennia old. We know that Go, the great game of China, was being played in 538BCE because it's described in the ancient narrative history book *Zuo Zhuan*.

Senet: an ancient contender

Senet and the Royal Game of Ur have all of those beaten. The earliest Royal Game of Ur boards date from around 2600BCE, at least 4,500 years ago, and Senet, also known as the "game of passing," is 500 years older than that. In fact, the Egyptian hieroglyphic for "passage" is a stylized Senet board—playing on dual meanings of players passing each other in play and, as the game took on spiritual significance, passage into the afterlife after death. There are games that are older, but since they were created before the human race could write, we have no way of knowing what they were called, how they were played, who played them, or why. But archeological digs in modern-day Jordan, Israel, Syria, Egypt, and Iran have unearthed boards made of limestone or gypsum, all with similar lines of round pits, some with decorations or extra marks. These appear to be game boards. Specifically, they look like the boards

The first board games that we know of were played 8,000 years ago.

Main image: Copy of an ancient painting (dated to the reign of Ramesses II, 1279–1213BCE) showing Queen Nefertari playing Senet, found on the side of Nefertari's tomb, Valley of the Queens, Thebes, Egypt. **Additional images:** Round counter pieces from Royal Game of Ur.

SENET • Year/period created: **3,100BCE** • Designer: **Ancient Egyptians** • Place of origin: **Egypt** • Number of players: **2–4** • Time to play: **Unknown** • Complexity: **Medium**

used to play Mancala (see pp.26–33) today. We have no idea if that's what they were, and no pieces have been found to go with them, but the oldest dates to at least 6000BCE. In other words, they're 8,000 years old.

Eight thousand years ago, brickmaking and alcohol were new inventions. The wheel, bronze, and taming horses were still thousands of years in the future. Yet these ancient people thought that these game boards were important enough to make them out of more permanent materials. They may have played other games, too, but those haven't survived the passage of time—at least not in their original form. Because games, even ones as old as this, do two remarkable things: they evolve, and they travel.

Pharaoh of Egypt Tutankhamun was a gamer. The game Senet was so important to him that he was buried with four different sets of it, ranging from an ornate table version to a slim travel set made of ivory. Nefertari, wife of Ramesses II, was also a Senet player. In one of the wall paintings in her lavishly decorated tomb in the Valley of the Queens, she is shown sitting at a Senet board, playing against an opponent who is not in the picture. Senet had many meanings for the Egyptians, but by the time of Tutankhamun and Nefertari, it had become associated with the journey through the afterlife. Some Egyptian writings say that as part of this journey, the dead would have to play the game against a divine opponent.

The rules of Senet have been lost, but we know a lot about how the game was played thanks to Egyptian texts that describe games in progress. These include the first recorded example of trash talk, between two Senet players who appear painted on the wall of the tomb of the provincial governor Pepiankh in Meir. The first player taunts his opponent:

"It [the game piece] has alighted. Be happy my heart, for I shall cause you to see it taken away ..."

WRITING ON THE WALL OF THE TOMB OF PEPIANKH

The iconic image of Death playing chess may have started with Egyptian writings on the subject of playing games against a divine opponent.

Senet and Ur were played by Egyptian royalty.

Senet remained for the most part unchanged for 3,000 years but originally had seven pieces per side, not five.

Senet space number 27 — the House of Water — sends any piece that lands on it back to the middle of the track. Players need to throw an exact number to move off the board.

Senet board

The "House of Water"

The second player then replies, "You speak as one weak of tongue, for passing is mine."

Working from these descriptions and fragments, historian R. C. Bell and archeologist Dr. Timothy Kendall have assembled the most complete version of the rules of the game. There are two important things to know about it. First, even the most complicated version—Kendall's—is still very simple by modern standards. And second, it's not a very good game. It's fiddly, too random, and lacking in either tactics or tension.

Senet, like many early board games, is a race. Each player has a team of five pieces and throws casting sticks to get a random number (dice hadn't been invented yet) to move them, trying to get them all to the end of the board, jockeying for position and bumping their opponent's pieces backward. A piece on its own is vulnerable, but two together are protected, so you have to keep your forces together. Some spaces on the board are good; some are bad.

Conical pieces

Spool-shaped pieces

Left: Wooden Senet board from approximately 1550–1295BCE.

And yet these rules alone do not produce a satisfying game, and that doesn't make sense. Senet was played in Egypt for 3,000 years, twice as long as Chess has existed. It was played by pharaohs, priests, dentists, and masons alike. Either the game was being used for some other purpose than recreation or gambling, or we're missing something important about how it should work. In other words, the reconstructed rules are almost certainly incorrect or incomplete.

You can buy Senet sets. Many of them are beautiful objects, modeled on Egyptian originals, lovely to look at. And to be honest, that's probably a better use for them than trying to play the game.

ROYAL GAME OF UR • Year/period created: *2600BCE* • Designer: *Mesopotamians*
Place of origin: *Middle East* • Number of players: *2* • Time to play: *Unknown* • Complexity: *Medium*

The Royal Game of Ur: stealing the lead

So if Senet is not the oldest game that we can play in its original form, then what is? The answer, thanks to an extraordinary piece of academic detective work, is the Royal Game of Ur, also known as the Game of 20 Squares. It was a popular and widespread game. The Senet sets found in Tutankhamun's tomb are double-sided: if you flip them over, there's a board for the Royal Game on the back.

The Royal Game of Ur takes its name from the cemetery where archeologist Sir Leonard Woolley excavated five sets in the 1920s. Ur was one of the most important city-states in Mesopotamia, a center for trade, and there was something about this game that was more accessible or enjoyable to people from other cultures. Game boards have been found as far away as Crete to the west and Kochi in India to the east. But, like so many ancient games, the rules seem to be lost, and although archeologists have speculated about the meanings of the symbols on the boards, their work is mostly guesses.

We'd still be in the dark if not for Dr. Irving Finkel of the British Museum. Dr Finkel is a leading authority on cuneiform, the early Sumerian system of writing inscribed into clay tablets, and also an enthusiastic games researcher and player. He organized the conference in 1990 that's credited with kick-starting the whole field of ancient games research. And it was Dr. Finkel who realized that an obscure tablet that had been in the British Museum archives since 1880, along with 130,000 others, was not a system for fortune-telling or the names of dogs, but the rules of a game.

Thanks to his research, the boards of the Royal Game of Ur have been reunited with what are almost certainly their original rules.

The Royal Game of Ur was played with astragals—knucklebones of a sheep—to give a number betwen one and four. Versions with tetrahedral (four-sided) dice have also been found.

Right: Babylonian tablet from 177–176BCE, measuring less than 3½in (9cm) across, translated by Dr. Irving Finkel. Rules for the Game of Ur were engraved in Sumerian cuneiform, in columns.

Hound and Jackal pins

These rules show that Ur is in fact a good game! It's still dominated by the results of random throws, but it's a tense and exciting race for two players, as their pieces enter on opposite sides of the board, merge onto a shared path where they jostle for position and special spaces, and then divide again to exit the board. This was more than a simple race game. The Royal Game of Ur had systems for gambling baked into its rules, as well as connections to astrological constellations.

Left: Royal Game of Ur board with round and tetrahedral gaming pieces from 2600BCE.

The Egyptians also played Hounds and Jackals, a race game with ornate pieces and a probable gambling element, and Mehen, a game with a board shaped like a coiled snake.

Like most ancient games, the Royal Game seemed to die out, and nobody is sure why. There are theories that it evolved into Backgammon, or was supplanted by it. The two games have similarities, but Backgammon has more strategy. Other theories suggest most games do not survive the demise of the cultures that created them. But it turns out that the Royal Game had not died completely. Dr. Finkel discovered that a Jewish community in the Indian city of Kochi had been playing a recognizable version of the game for generations. He was able to track down someone who remembered playing the game as a child and described playing it with rules very similar to the ones he had deciphered from the clay tablet.

Fans of Go (see p.28) like to claim that it's the game that's been played continuously for the longest time, but, thanks to Dr. Finkel, the Royal Game of Ur has beaten it by a millennium. We may not understand the significance of the Royal Game today, or use its systems to gamble, but we can still enjoy its tense play, the thrills of victory, and the sweet pain of seeing a piece sent back to the start and feel the same way that ancient Sumerian scribes and the kings and queens of Ur did when they played it.

Mehen turtle votive

Games without Frontiers

Games are something that almost every human culture has invented.

Mesopotamia may have been the birthplace of board games, but Indian cultures were playing dice games as far back as 2,300BCE. The African game Mancala can be dated to around 500BCE, and China began to develop its own games in the same era. Meanwhile in the Americas, the Mayans were playing race games in the 7th century, and we can never know how old the Aztec game of Patolli is because the invading Europeans destroyed all the records of that culture.

Multi-versioned Mancala

Early games were often simple race games based mostly on chance. They were considered to have a connection to divination, as good luck and the future were in the hands of the gods. Games went on to evolve with different rules and variants, sometimes even becoming new games in their own right. The idea of a game having fixed rules is quite new, and often wrong. Even modern classics like Carcassonne (see p.133) have varying rules and point scores. One of the best early examples of this is Mancala.

   The name refers not to one game but to an extended family of games that originated in North Africa and spread along ancient migration, trade, and slave routes to reach India, Southeast Asia, the Caribbean, and South

There are almost 1,000 known versions of Mancala with more than 800 different names, from Abangah to Wa-wee.

Mancala is unlike many folk games, which usually do not have a theme.

Main image: Section from a Japanese woodblock triptych from c.1893 titled "The Feminine Accomplishments of Tea and the Game of Go." *Additional images:* Round Game of Go pieces on their square, checked board.

America. It's thought that the game originated in Egypt around 1,000BCE, but the origins of this evidence are unclear. Ancient boards with a remarkable similarity to Mancala boards (two rows of six holes) have been excavated in Jordan, but we have no information beyond that. Today's game most likely came from the ancient Kingdom of Aksum, in what is now Ethiopia and Eritrea, around 1,500 years ago.

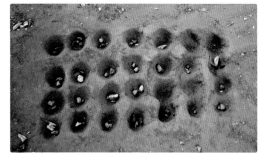

Mancala markings carved in the ground

Mancala has no standard set of rules, or even a standard board. Boards can have anywhere from 12 to 40 holes, up to 400 counters, and hundreds of rule variations. Despite this variety, all Mancala games have the same basic format: two players take turns sowing small objects (usually nuts, seeds, beads, or pebbles) in rows of holes. It's a fast, themed folk game all about farming: sowing, harvesting, and stealing crops.

Mancala looks deceptively simple and is very much a game of tactics and skill. To make it even more challenging, it's usually played quickly, with each player ready to go the moment the other finishes. In African marketplaces and street cafés, it can draw excited, noisy crowds. In Ghanaian Owari, the game's most popular version, the board has two rows of six holes and a larger pit at each end. Play begins with four seeds in each hole. The first player chooses a hole on their side, takes all the seeds from it, and places them in other holes in a structured way. Circumstance can cause them to lose seeds or enable them to harvest their partner's. Whoever gains a majority of the seeds is the winner. Mancala is still played widely across Africa, possibly because it's not hard to scratch out a board and find pebbles or beans. Also, the rules are easy to teach, and play is fast and fun. Success or failure is not in the lap of the gods but is down to skill. And maybe sometimes a little cheating.

Ornately carved wooden boards are a traditional wedding gift (or a souvenir for tourists), sometimes with cowrie shells or semiprecious stones as playing pieces.

MANCALA • Year/period created: **500–600CE** • Place of origin: **Africa** • Number of players: **2** • Time to play: **10 minutes** • Complexity: **Medium**

The great game of Go

China's board-game traditions began at least 2,500 years ago with a game called Go. According to legend, the game was created by the semimythical Emperor Yao to instruct his son, which has led to stories that it's more than 4,000 years old, but the earliest proven reference dates it only as far back as 548BCE. Over the next thousand years, the game spread to Korea and Japan, possibly via Tibet. Go has a 19x19 square grid, but its original 17x17 one is still used by Tibetans today.

Go is the game's Japanese name. The Chinese called it "Yi," and later on "Weiqi," which means "surrounding board game."

Go stones are referred to as "alive," "dead," or "unsettled."

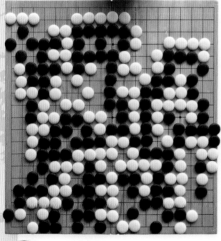

Modern Go board and pieces

Go is not a folk game; its valuable board and pieces put it in the domain of nobles and scholars.

One of 181 black stones and 180 white stones

The simple and elegant display of white and black stones on the square grid disguises the complex interplay between the two sides. On your turn, you place a stone of your color anywhere on the board, trying to surround areas of space or the other player's stones. Once a stone is placed, it doesn't move unless it's surrounded—and captured. The player with the most territory at the end wins.

Go appears simple and is fast to learn, and it's better than Chess—harder, subtler, more beautiful. That's not just opinion; it's a demonstrable fact. In 1997, the best Chess player in the world, Garry Kasparov, was beaten by IBM's Deep Blue computer in a six-game Chess tournament. But it took another 19 years for an artificial intelligence to defeat the finest Go player, Mr. Lee Sedol of South Korea. The computer AlphaGo (created by the Google project Deepmind) had to evolve a new style of play. This different approach is partly mathematics. In Go, you can play a piece anywhere on the 19x19 board; in Chess, you are limited by a smaller board and each piece's steps. Thus, Chess has 20 opening moves, whereas Go has 361. The human mind cannot plan strategy that far ahead. Instead, you have to think in terms of patterns and blocks, of which areas of the board you can control and defend.

GO • Year/period created: **548BCE** • Designer: **Rumored to be Emperor Yao** • Place of origin: **China** • Number of players: **2** • Time to play: **20–90 minutes, but tournament games last hours** • Complexity: **Medium**

Most games evolve from earlier games, but there's no evidence of Go having been influenced by others, and it seems incredible that one of the greatest games ever created sprang from the mind of a single person. However, Go's brilliance is in the complex strategy that emerges from the interplay of a few simple rules. And it does seem possible that one person could create a grid, place black and white stones on it, find it fun to surround an opponent's pieces, spot a few situations that need extra rules, and thus discover the complete game in front of them. Perhaps it really was Emperor Yao. We'll never know.

Japanese porcelain model of Chinese children playing the Game of Go from 18th century

Racing on cross-shaped boards

India has a long history of games, but little information has survived, and much is difficult to date accurately. Traditionally, most Indian game boards were made of painted or embroidered cloth, which disintegrates over time. However, we do know that more than 4,000 years ago, the Bronze Age Harappan civilization in the Indus Valley in South Asia was using cubic and rectangular dice to roll numbers between one and four.

We mainly know about Indian games because they were written about, such as in the epic poem *Mahabharata*, parts of which date back to 500BCE. The central figure, Yudhisthira, is tricked into a gambling game, possibly a version of Pachisi or Chaupar. Because his high status means he cannot refuse the challenge, he is cheated out of all his possessions, ultimately including his wife Draupadi. In one version, he loses because the dice are magic, made from the bones of an adversary's father.

The most solid reference to Pachisi and Chaupar comes from Emperor Akbar I, who died in 1605, nearly 2,000 years after the *Mahabharata*. He built human-sized boards of marble in his many palaces. Slaves were the pieces, and they wore team colors, while the players sat on a raised dais.

Both Pachisi and Chaupar are race games for up to four players, or two pairs of players, played on a cross-shaped board. Players throw sticks or dice to move, aiming to get all their four pieces around the edge of the board and home. But Pachisi and Chaupar are more aggressive than

The oldest dice in the world were discovered in the ruins of the Burnt City in Iran, dated to before 2500BCE.

Games of Chaupar could last for days!

Painted wooden Pachisi pawn, sometimes moved with wooden sticks

PACHISI • Year/period created: *16th century* • Place of origin: *India* • Number of players: *2–4* • Time to play: *30–60 minutes* • Complexity: *Medium*

Women playing Pachisi, seated on a patterned floor spread, from 1725

Pawns in the form of an Indian lady, from 1725

Cloth Pachisi board

earlier race games; movement has to be forward, but much of the enjoyment comes from hunting down other players' undefended pieces.

In the West, Pachisi is known through its dumbed-down offspring. These poor relations were brought to the UK in 1863 as Ludo and to the US in 1867 as Parcheesi. All the strategy from the sophisticated original was swapped for dice rolling. Gone were the special moves, the system for hunting other players' pieces and strategies for protecting your own pieces. Much of the enjoyment of Pachisi and Chaupar came from this hunting of undefended pieces, which made the race games more aggressive than earlier ones.

A piece of holy scripture from around 500BCE holds some clues for dating these Indian games. In the *Digha Nikaya*, Buddha lays down principles for living a devout life. Among them is a list of games that he said he would not play, and therefore his followers should not play either. No specific game is named, but dice games are out, as are any played on a board of eight or 10 rows (this would include Senet and the Royal Game of Ur, which could have made their way to India by this time). Also forbidden is a game that sounds like a distant ancestor of Pictionary, one that involves playing games in your mind, and a selection of specific items such as toy plows and windmills made from palm leaves.

These religious teachings tell us that by the 5th century BCE, board games were widespread and well known, but what's more, they were seen as a negative on the path to enlightenment. Despite their origins in ritual, games would continue to run into trouble with organized religion, from bans on gambling to the "Satanic Panic" around Dungeons & Dragons (see p.122) in the late 1970s. But at least we can use this disapproval as a way of dating some Indian games.

On the other side of the world from India, the Aztecs in Central America also created a cross-shaped race game, which they called Patolli. We cannot age Patolli because, although the Aztec Empire existed from 1325 to 1521, the game may have evolved from earlier ones played by tribes in North America.

While Pachisi's boards fell to the ravages of time, Patolli's boards were lost to ravages of the conquering Spanish. However, drawings of them by Spanish historians look remarkably like Pachisi boards, and the description of the game play is very similar, too: players race multiple pieces around the edge of the board, gambling on the outcome. Some historians have become very excited, insisting that these similarities mean there must have been contact between the two cultures. However, this hasn't been proven, and in games creation, we do often see similar ideas arising independently in different places. After all, there is only a finite number of things that can be done with dice and counters. (Although you may be surprised!)

Right: A painting from the 16th-century *Rasamanjari* (Essence of the Experience of Delight), a Sanskrit love poem by Bhanudatta, depicts a game of Chaupar that has led to an argument. Parvati pleads with her husband, Shiva, who has cheated a necklace from her as part of the game.
Left: A game resembling Patolli appears on pages of the Aztec Codex Mendoza, dated to 1540, which suggests that the Aztecs greatly valued the game.

"The greedy do not get success ...
When in danger, sacrifice ...
Against strong positions, play safe."

TRANSLATION FROM JI XIN WANG'S TANG-DYNASTY GOLDEN RULES OF GO

Games Afoot

When the Romans arrived, games went global.

The Romans were keen games players, and they mostly played for recreation rather than for any ritual or religious reason. They were risk-takers and gamblers—even though there were laws against gambling. They were also conquerors and traders. Their soldiers and merchants carried the games they loved across the whole of their empire and sometimes beyond. But the Romans were also borrowers who were influenced by the cultures that they encountered, assimilating everything from mythology to architecture into the Roman world, and games were no exception.

Men's Morris out and about

The Romans left plentiful evidence of their love of games, much of it on their architecture, with game boards carved into the walls of buildings. Sometimes these would be official carvings for popular games, often inscribed with the name of the person who had donated the funds to pay for it. More often, they would be unofficial scratchings. At Aphrodisias, a late Roman city in southern Turkey, there are more than 100 boards for different games, many of them carved in flagstones around bath houses.

The most common design in Aphrodisias is a circle divided into eight segments: the board for Three Men's Morris. Three is the smallest of the Morris games; the other members of the family are Six, Nine, and Twelve. Nine Men's Morris is the most common, and its boards can be found carved into the stone seats, flagstones, and roof tiles of medieval buildings across Europe.

Twelve Men's Morris is still popular in South Africa, Botswana, and Lesotho, where it's called Morabaraba.

Main image: Painted wooden version of Nine Men's Morris board game showing the game traveled as far as Germany. Dated to approximately 1500CE, and held in the Bavarian National Museum, Munich. *Additional images:* Details from Nine Men's Morris board.

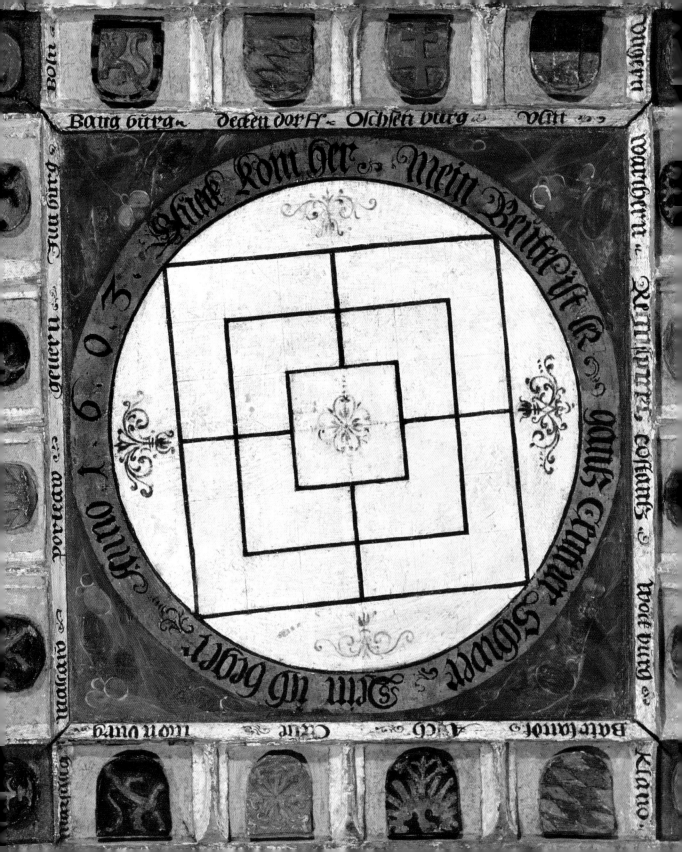

NINE MEN'S MORRIS • Year/period created: **Roman, potentially 1400BCE** • Place of origin: **Roman Empire** • Number of players: **2** • Time to play: **Up to an hour** • Complexity: **Low**

Left: The Romans scratched Nine Men's Morris boards onto whatever surfaces were available, including stone walls and floors.

Each higher-numbered version has more pieces and therefore a larger, more complicated board than lower-numbered games, but Men's Morris was very much a folk game—even the board for Twelve Men's Morris can be made in a few seconds by drawing three squares and eight straight lines.

Morris is the English name for the game. It may be Shakespeare's name for it—its earliest use seems to be in *A Midsummer Night's Dream* (1595/1596). The fairy queen Titania says, "The Nine Men's Morris is filled up with mud." Across Europe, it also goes by Mills, Double Mills, and hundreds of different names, most of them sounding a lot like merellus— the Roman word for a game piece.

All versions of the game work the same way: you try to get three of your pieces into a straight line, and if you succeed, then you remove one of your opponent's. If this sounds familiar, you've probably played *Candy Crush* or *Bejeweled*, which have a very similar match-three game mechanic at their core. There's something in the human mind that has found making lines of three deeply satisfying for thousands of years. The Morris games descend from Tic-Tac-Toe (or Noughts and Crosses), which was played in Egypt as far back as 1300BCE, but is a pastime that most players quickly outgrow. Noughts and Crosses also evolved into a Roman version called *Terni Lapilli* (Three Pebbles). It's played on the same nine-square grid with the same strategy, but instead of making marks, you place or move one of your three stones. These games were easily taught, easily remembered, and could be played anywhere, so as the Roman Empire sent its military and its traders around the world, the various merellus games went with them and found new players.

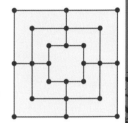

Three Men's Morris

Nine Men's Morris

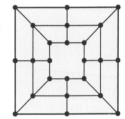

Twelve Men's Morris

Above: Sketches show the various setups of game boards in the Morris family.

Terni Lapilli—a descendant of Noughts and Crosses—has been played for millennia, using whatever objects were available.

36

Above: The 13th-century Spanish work *Libro de los Juegos* ("Book of Games") depicts Nine Men's Morris being played much farther afield than Italy, and with dice.

Searching for Twelve Marks

The Morris games spread the farthest of all the Roman games, but there were many others. Games were a key part of everyday Roman social interaction. There was the Game of Brigands/Little Soldiers (*Ludus Latrunculorum*), where players work to capture each other's pieces by trapping them between two of their own stones. This seems similar to an ancient Greek game, Petteia, though its rules have been lost and modern attempts to reconstruct them are based on very little. It may have been a forerunner of Checkers or hunt games like Hnefatafl (see p.48).

The Romans also enjoyed the Game of Twelve Marks (*Ludus Duodecim Scriptorum*). The game actually has 36 marks—or spaces—in three lines of 12 with a gap in the middle. Players moved their counters along these

37

lines, probably gambling on the outcome. Many boards use words to mark out the playing area, each letter forming one space on the board. Often the words refer to gaming, luck, celebrations, military victories, or the Roman circus. For example: *VICTUS LEBATE* (Loser, beat it!); *LUDERE NESCIS* (You cannot play); *DALUSO RI/LOCU(M)* (Let a real player take your place); *PARTHI OCCISI* (The Parthians are slain); *BRITTO VICTUS* (The Britons are defeated), or *LUDITE ROMANI* (Play, Romans!). Words found on boards outside a tavern include *HABEMUS INCENA* (We have dinner); *PULLUM, PISCEM* (Chicken, Fish) and *PERNAM, PAONEM* (Ham, Peacock).

Sadly, the rules for the Game of Twelve Marks haven't survived, though we do know that it was played with three dice and 15 pieces. This is very similar to another dice game called Alea, which later evolved into the Backgammon-like game Tabula. Thanks to the great Roman poet Ovid, we also know that play may not always have been focused on the board.

Ovid is remembered for his poetry, but several of his books are self-help manuals dealing with ways to apply cosmetics or get over a broken heart. His most popular, *Ars Amatoria* from c.8CE, was a three-volume manual on love and seduction. The first two volumes advise young men on how to approach women, and the third volume advises women on how to deal with men who have read the first two. They're flippant and funny, filled with classical allegory and wit. And they suggest that a casual game or two is a good way to get into someone's affections. Ovid describes (but doesn't name) games he thinks suitable for this purpose. Two of the descriptions sound like Three Men's Morris and the Game of Twelve Marks. Ovid writes, "Many a time, while playing, is love commenced. But the least matter is how to use the throws to advantage;

Above: Stone game carving from Aphrodisias Anatolia, Turkey, Asia Minor.

Many Game of Twelve Marks boards have survived, partly because the heavy stones were often later used to cover tombs in catacombs.

Emperor Nero apparently had small ivory chariots for Tabula and gambled up to 400,000 sesterces a time. This was the minimum a person had to own in property to be part of the equites (knight) class.

'tis a task of greater consequence to lay a restraint on one's manners. While we are not thinking, and are revealed by our very intentness, and, through the game, our feelings, laid bare, are exposed; anger arises, a disgraceful failing, and the greed for gain; quarrels, too, and strife, and, then, bitter regrets. Recriminations are uttered; the air resounds with the brawl, and every one for himself invokes the angry Divinities."

"'Tis shocking for the fair one not to know how to play."

OVID IN *ARS AMATORIA*

Whether or not Roman games typically ended in a fight—which is surely not the way to win your crush's heart—this was the first civilization where playing games pervaded every level of life. Games were everywhere, from spectacles and gladiatorial combats in the arena to competitions at home, in public, or on the road. And they were enjoyed by everyone, from the lowest level of society to the highest, including emperors, many of whom were inveterate gamblers.

It takes more than the decline and fall of an empire to stop merchants from plying their trade, so games continued to make their way around the world, but this process slowed down without the legions from Rome bringing games and eager players to far-flung colonies. Evidence becomes hazy as to where the next games originated from, but it's out of the following dark age that three of the best-known games in the history of the world emerge: Checkers (Draughts), Backgammon, and Chess.

Above: Bookplate for a 1644 edition of Ovid's *Ars Amatoria*.

Right: Ettore Ferrari's statue of the Roman poet Ovid, created in 1887, stands in front of the National History and Archeological Museum in the Romanian Black Sea port of Constanta, where Ovid died in 17CE.

Check Please

The origins of some of the world's greatest games—Chess and Backgammon—are still concealed in the mists of time and the subject of fierce argument among historians.

There is a branch of academia devoted to studying the history of board games. Books on this topic have been published since the Victorian era, and, more recently, the International Board Game Studies Association was established with the purpose of researching and debating this topic. The origins of Chess and Backgammon have been hotly contested over the years. The fact that Chess and Backgammon resemble one another does not necessarily mean they share a common history. Chess is believed to have originated in India, whereas several countries claim to be the birthplace of Backgammon. Let's investigate further ...

In Senet and Backgammon, the player moves pieces along a board, using random numbers to determine how far to move. They can capture opposing pieces by landing on them, or protect their own by guarding them.

Backgammon's backstory

Backgammon is one of the few games to remain almost unchanged for more than 1,000 years, but its origins go back even further. There could be tenuous links to the game of Senet from Ancient Egypt—but while the two race games have some similarities, they're very different in design and play. In addition, almost every culture where games were created had something similar, for example, Pachisi was played in India, and Liubo has its roots in China. Can these games be ancestors of Backgammon? Online theorists would have you believe they could be. The game's origins are muddled, and there's no way of knowing the whole truth.

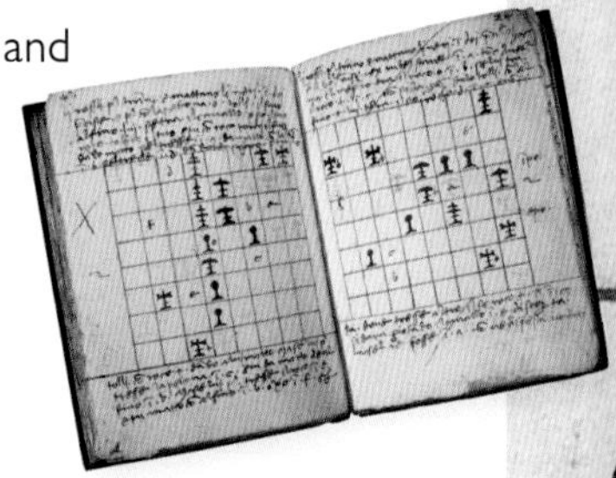

Main image: Alfonso X, king of León, Galicia, and Castile, commissioned *Libro de los Juegos*, an illustrated book of games, around the year 1282. It shows 14 competing versions of the game Nard. One of these is almost identical to modern Backgammon, as depicted here.

Additional images: Illustrated Italian 15th-century Chess manual.

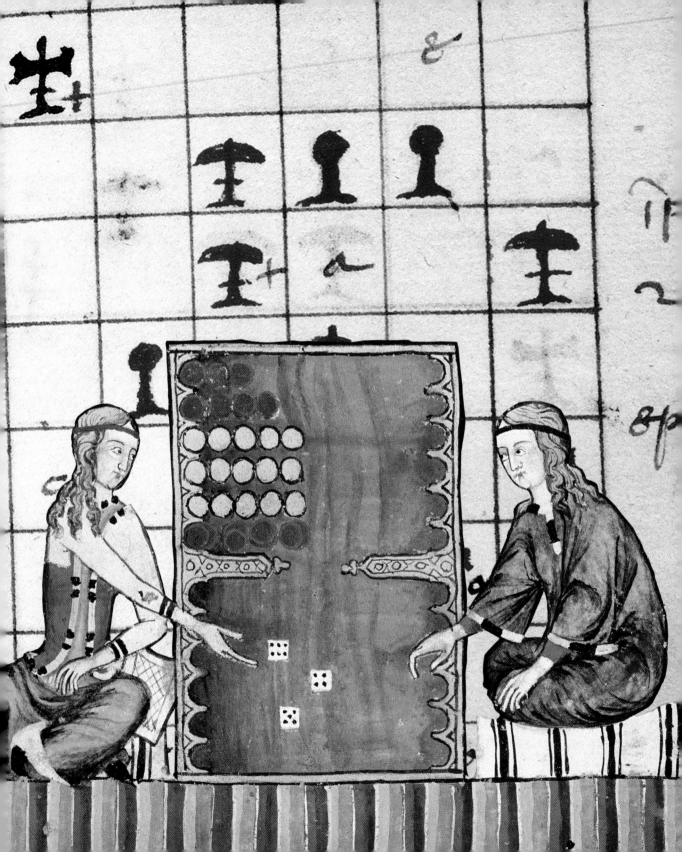

BACKGAMMON • Year/period created: **600CE** • Designer: **Possibly Buzurgmihr** • Number of players: **2** • Time to play: **5–60 minutes** • Complexity: **Medium**

Place of origin: **Possibly Iran**

A two-player race game, Backgammon is played on a board with 24 spaces. The players move their 15 pieces—checkers—in opposite directions along a track. Two dice dictate how many spaces a player can move each turn: the player chooses whether to use the whole roll on one checker or to split the roll to move two checkers. A single checker on a space is unprotected and is sent to the middle of the board if the opponent's checker lands on it. The first player to "bear off" all their checkers, taking them off the board, wins the game.

The origins of Backgammon are intertwined with myths from different nations. The main contenders are Ancient Rome, Persia (now Iran), and India. Other claims can be discounted fairly easily. For example, western traditions claim that Backgammon was created during the Trojan War, possibly by the Greek soldier Palamedes, who also apparently invented dice and the alphabet. Needless to say, there's no evidence for this.

Persian legend claims that the Indian King Devaśarman sent a Chess set without rules to King Khusrau I of Iran, to test the wisdom of his advisors. Not only did Khusrau's advisor Buzurgmihr figure out the game and defeat the Indian envoy in three matches, but he also devised a new game—Noble-is-Ardashir—filled with Zoroastrian symbolism. Buzurgmihr took his game to India where Devaśarman's advisors could not decipher its meaning and were disgraced. Noble-is-Ardashir, it's thought, was

Backgammon. It's a great story, however, we know Backgammon (or at least Nard, its Middle Eastern predecessor) was around centuries before Khusrau ruled in the 6th century. Secondly, the chance a first-timer could create a game as polished as Backgammon in a few days is remote.

A Backgammon board with 15 white and 15 black checkers.

Always associated with rulers, Backgammon didn't acquire its modern, aristocratic style until the 1960s, when Russian Prince Alexis Obolensky popularized it.

Prince Alexis Obolensky cofounded the World Backgammon Club in 1967, with tournaments held annually.

Backgammon additions, such as the doubling die—which makes betting on the game either more interesting or more hazardous—didn't arrive until the 20th century.

Japan's Ban-Sugoroku and China's Shuanglu are very similar to modern Backgammon.

Tracking Tabula and Nard

Perhaps Backgammon's roots can be traced back to the Roman game of Tabula. Played on a 24-space board, it evolved from the *Duodecim Scriptora* (Game of Twelve Marks; see p.25) board, with the middle row removed. Although Tabula used three dice instead of two and all pieces began the game off the board, modern Backgammon players would recognize much of it.

Tabula was popular in Rome and across its empire from the 1st century. Emperor Claudius was said to have had a board fixed to his chariot so he could play as he traveled, and there are verses commemorating a legendarily awful dice throw made by the Byzantine Emperor Zeno around 475 CE. It must have been bad if people are still talking about it a millennium and a half later.

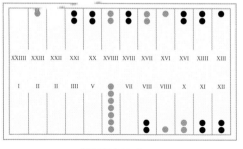

Tabula board

While Tabula remained in Europe, the Romans were trading with the Middle East. This explains how the game reached Persia, where it evolved into Nard in around the 3rd century. As "Nardshir," it seems to have traveled to India, where it was claimed as a local invention, and then on to China, where it was regarded as an Indian game, and then across most of Asia and parts of Africa.

CHESS • Year/period created: **6th century CE** • Designer: **Unknown** • Place of origin: **Northwest India**
Number of players: **2** • Time to play: **1–3 hours** • Complexity: **Hard**

Like Tabula, Nard is a recognizable version of the Backgammon we know today. It also used 15 counters per player and a board very similar to the one used in modern Backgammon, though the rules and the start position of the pieces were different. Nard also had the players start at opposite ends of the board, with pieces already in place, running the same course in the same direction. Hundreds of years later, Nard came to Europe, bringing these innovations back with it. It arrived as part of the Moorish conquest of Spain and in the backpacks of soldiers returning from the Crusades.

Above: Modern-day Chess set with pieces in play.

Chasing Chess

The origins of Chess are a little less convoluted. Chess is the great game, the benchmark against which all others are judged. It's taught in schools, its high-profile tournaments are televised, and its grandmasters are household names (in a particular sort of household). Chess is the game that people think of as a sign of intelligence and strategy. Its terms have passed into everyday language: pawns, gambit, endgame, checkmate, and stalemate. It's been the basis for many works of art and literature, and it can exercise a fanatical dedication in its followers—take Dada artist Marcel Duchamp, who in 1923 abandoned art and devoted all his time to playing Chess, rising to the rank of "Chess master."

Above: The Lewis Chess pieces were carved from walrus ivory and whales' teeth, and probably made in Trondheim, Norway, around 1150–1200CE.

Left: This almost complete Chess set from Iran is one of the earliest extant examples in the world, dating from the 12th century. The pieces are abstract forms: the shah (king) is represented as a throne; the vizier (the equivalent of the queen) is a smaller throne.

It's generally agreed that Chess comes from India, where it developed from the 6th-century game of Chaturanga. It was a two-player game, with an 8x8 square board. Each player began with a row of pawns and behind them a raja (king) attended by a mantri (vizier), and on either side of them two elephants, two horses, and two chariots. Each type of piece could move only in a particular way, pieces were removed from the game by "swap-taking", and the game ended when one of the rajas was neutralized. This is not precisely Chess as we know it, but it's very close.

Chaturanga arose in northwest India, and the likely date of its creation coincides with the story of the Persian and Indian kings and Buzurgmihr inventing Backgammon. If there's any truth to that story, it would make sense that Chaturanga was a new game that hadn't yet spread outside India, so nobody in Persia had yet seen it. The Persians took to the game, calling it Shatranj and introducing their own modifications. From there, it spread west into Europe and east where it evolved into similar Chess-like games.

Where did Chaturanga come from? The board was originally used to play Ashtapada, an old Indian race game that was referred to on the list of games that Buddha declined to play (see p.31). The arrangement of pieces was very similar to an actual Indian battle formation known as an akshauhini, described in the epic *Mahabharata*. Two of the smallest units belonging to the akshauhini—patti—had two elephants, two chariots, six horses, and 10 foot soldiers—close to the number of pieces in Chaturanga.

Chess was the inspiration for *Through the Looking-Glass* (1871) by Lewis Carroll, and *The Luzhin Defense* (1930), by novelist Vladimir Nabokov, who also had a sideline in creating Chess problems.

Ivory Bishop piece, 8th–10th century

Jet Pawn piece, 8th–10th century

Jet Knight piece, 8th–10th century

Some people claim that Chaturanga was a variation on another game played on the Ashtapada board: Chaturaji, a four-player gambling game with kings, elephants, and horses, and where dice or throwing sticks determined which piece to move next. The noted games historian R. C. Bell believed this was the original ancestor of Chess, but it's not mentioned in any writings until about 1030CE and doesn't seem to have been widely played.

Indian Chess board

None of this explains where one of the most characteristic elements of Chess came from: the checkered board. It turns out that this is one of Europe's two major contributions to the game along with replacing the vizier with the queen—and later making her the most powerful piece on the board. Both checkered boards and queens made their first appearance in the *Einsiedeln verses*, the earliest written references to Chess in Europe, dating back to 997CE.

However, the queen piece retained the short moves of Chaturanga's vizier until 1200, where she gained a jump on her first move, and then around 1500 in Spain, she became the superpowered game changer in a version known variously as "Queen's Chess" or "Madwoman's Chess."

All of this makes it sound as if there was one version of Chess, occasionally updated, but that wasn't the case at all. There was no agreed version. Every country and region had its own variations, from the size of the board to the role of the pieces. In Alfonso X's *Libro de los Juegos,* there are descriptions of "Great Chess," played on a 12x12 board, as well as "Four Seasons Chess" with four players, looking similar to Chaturaji, and "Decimal Chess" played with seven-sided dice.

This also reinforces the point that Chess, like Backgammon, was not a folk game, not something you could scratch out on the ground and play with pebbles while watching the sheep. It was the domain of the elite. Ordinary people could not afford a Chess set with 32 different carved pieces (48 for Great Chess) and a special board. They would have to find their fun elsewhere.

Another theory for the invention of Chaturanga involves a general in the army of King Devaśarman seeking to train his officers in strategic thinking and then a set made from emeralds and rubies being sent to the King of Persia.

Above: Early queen Chess piece, from 13th-century Scandinavia, riding a horse to battle and surrounded by an entourage.

In 1968, Marcel Duchamp played Chess on stage against the composer John Cage with a specially made board. Each move triggered a photoelectric cell that produced music.

Above: Hindu god Krishna is depicted playing Chess against a woman from Koksara, India, in one of a sequence of gouache illustrations.

"I wouldn't mind being a Pawn, if only I might join—though of course I should like to be a Queen, best."

ALICE, IN LEWIS CARROLL'S *THROUGH THE LOOKING-GLASS*

Two Times Table

Across medieval northern Europe, new games sailed onto the scene as Vikings and Saxons conquered lands and scholars turned to higher, mathematical pursuits.

A lot of the games played in early medieval Europe derived from either those brought by the Romans or those that had arrived from Persia and India. However, northern Europe was beginning to develop its own games, and particularly a family of games known as Tafl. The word "tafl" means "table" or "board," making it another game named after this piece of furniture—like the Roman game Tabula, but this time it's the game of the Vikings and Saxons.

Game of Tafl

Interestingly, Tafl is unlike any game that has come before it. There are elements of Chess and the Roman *Ludus Latrunculorum* (Game of Brigands/Little Soldiers) in its play, but the link is a tenuous one. Tafl is an early war game, and it's asymmetric—meaning two players have teams of different sizes and there are different ways of winning. One player is the attacker, starting with a large force around the edges of the board; the second player is the defender, with half as many pieces. The defender's pieces are arranged at the center, with the king in the middle. The attacker wins by surrounding the king with four pieces (two in some versions and reconstructions of the rules); the defender wins if they can get their king to the edge of the board. There are several Tafl games, with boards ranging in size from 7x7 squares, to a vast 19x19!

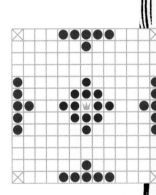

Above: Hnefatafl begins with 24 attacking pieces and 12 defending pieces, with the king in the center.

Main image: Medieval 14th-century illustration of a "lady and youth" playing Checkers.
Additional images: Wood and bone Alquerque pieces from Scandinavia in the 13th century. This early version of Checkers (or Draughts) traveled from North Africa to Spain and then on to the rest of Europe.

TAFL • Year/period created: **pre-500CE** • Designer: **Unknown** • Place of origin: **Scandinavia**
Number of players: **2** • Time to play: **5–20 minutes** • Complexity: **Medium**

The most common variant in this family is Tafl, later known as Hnefatafl (pronounced huh-neva-tavul, meaning "King's table"). It probably dates from around the 6th century, possibly earlier. Invading Norsemen brought it to Iceland, Ireland, Wales, and England, where sets have been found in grand Saxon burials, including Sutton Hoo, and also parts of Russia. Unlike Senet, it didn't seem to have any strong religious significance: people may have been buried with it because they enjoyed playing it in life, or perhaps it was to give the dead something to do in the afterlife.

The precise rules of Tafl were not written down, but there are a few records of how it was played. Unlike the Romans, the Scandinavians were not renowned for their record keeping, but they were keen on sagas (epic stories of heroic achievements), and several include descriptions of Tafl games. Famed 12th-century Norwegian Rögnvald Kali Kolsson compiled a list of his top skills, or boasts, including "I am strong at hafl-play". A century later, the *Herverar* saga, part of the Norse sagas that inspired J. R. R. Tolkien's *The Lord of the Rings*, included these riddles:

Descriptions in the sagas tell of a Tafl player leaping to their feet and sending the pieces flying.

In the 10th century, some Tafl pieces were carved from whalebone.

Q. Who are the maids that fight weaponless around their lord, the brown ever sheltering and the fair ever attacking him?

A. The pieces in hnefatafl

Q. What is the beast all girdled in iron which kills the flocks? It has eight horns but no head?

A. The hnefi (king) in hnefatafl

Above: An ancient wooden board, found in Ballinderry, Ireland, dated around the 10th century, possibly used for Hnefatafl.

Although these are not the greatest jokes in history, this saga deals with the time before the settling of Iceland in 874CE, suggesting the game must have been played widely enough for people to understand riddles about it.

Above: A sketch of markings from a runestone in Ockelbo, Sweden, shows two players sitting with a Tafl board balanced on their knees.

The best description of how Tafl was played comes not from a saga or book of games but from the diaries of the Swedish botanist Carl Linnaeus. While traveling through Lapland in July 1732, he encountered the local Sámi people playing a game called Tablut—another word meaning board or table, like Tafl. Essentially a simpler version of Tafl, Tablut was played on a 9x9 board, with the defending army called the Swedes and the attackers called the Muscovites.

The rules of Tablut were simple and play was fast, but that doesn't mean it wasn't tactical. The defending player had a slight advantage, particularly if they could keep their forces together and capture attackers early. The game had died out almost everywhere by the 1800s but has been revived recently, and there is even an annual world championship.

Playing Rithmomachia by numbers

Less popular is another game from northern Europe, albeit from a few centuries later. Rithmomachia is one of the first games where we are reasonably sure we know the name of the inventor: an 11th-century Bavarian monk named Asilo of Würzburg. He used his game as a tool for demonstrating and teaching the principles of a theory of numbers created by the Roman mathematician Boethius five centuries earlier. Subsequently, scholars added to the rules, defining the size of the board and giving the game its name (Rithmomachia means "The Battle of the Numbers," although many refer to it as the less violent "Philosopher's Game"). Around 1090CE, all the different versions were codified into a single manuscript, probably by Benedictine monk Odo of Tournai, of Orléans.

This is a complex game, possibly the most complicated of all the early games. It has some similarities to Chess, partly since its board is two Chess boards joined together, but it is a significantly different game. Boethius had divided numbers into various different types, and each of the different playing piece shapes (round, square, triangular, and pyramids) are numbered according to one of the groups. One player is "odd" and one "even," and each player's pieces move depending on their shape.

Rithmomachia board

Some early writers attributed Rithmomachia to Greek philosopher Pythagoras.

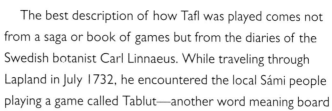

RITHMOMACHIA • Year/period created: **1030** • Designer: **Asilo of Würzburg** • Place of origin: **Northern Europe** • Number of players: **2** • Time to play: **Varies depending on rules used** • Complexity: **Hard**

When one piece comes into contact with another, it can take it in four possible ways: if it has the same value as the piece it's taking, for example, or if the player has surrounded the opposing piece with two pieces that add up to its value. On top of that, there are eight ways to win.

Rithmomachia is a mathematical thesis in the form of a board game, and to understand it, you need to know Boethius's theory. Rithmomachia was probably the first game created with a primarily educational purpose:

Above: Mathematician and philosopher Boethius pictured in an English manuscript dated 1150CE.

to teach the theory of numbers, and to encourage players to become more adept at mental arithmetic using Boethius's groups. It was certainly popular, moving out of the monastic realm into wider circles of universities and educated nobility across Europe.

For six centuries, Rithmomachia's combination of mathematics, philosophy, and education showed that games could be about more than recreation or gambling. However, sets were hard to come by, and it was difficult to find opponents to play it. As the field of mathematics changed and developed, Boethius's theories—along with the game itself—fell out of fashion. By the 1600s, the game had disappeared almost entirely and was largely forgotten for three centuries until scholars of medieval history began to find and collate references to it in old manuscripts.

Checkers vs. Draughts

The last of Europe's great medieval games is often overlooked, or dismissed as a childish pursuit that people learn and discard on their way to Chess or Backgammon. Confusingly, it has two different names in English. But this was the game that the settlers in New England played for a century and a half before taking up Chess, and it draws its American name from the board both games are played on—not a chessboard, but a "checkerboard." Checkers is the American name, Draughts in English, although it was

Rithmomachia reached England in the 13th century, where the philosopher Roger Bacon wrote of it, and later Sir Thomas More listed it among the recreational pursuits of the inhabitants of his *Utopia*.

Marion Tinsley (1927–1995) is considered to be the world's best Checkers player of his time, losing just seven games in a career spanning 45 years!

Modern Checkers board and pieces

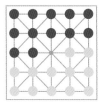

Above: Starting position for a game of Alquerque with 12 pieces for each player.

originally "chekyrs" in Old English. The name Draughts came later, from the way the pieces were pushed, not lifted, to move them. It's not the only game where pieces could move only forwards, but it's the most notable one, and it's a splendid game in its own right.

At some point (probably around 1100CE), somewhere in Europe (possibly southern France), someone took the checkers from a Backgammon set, laid them out on a chessboard, and started pushing them around using the moves of a little-known capturing game called Alquerque, or Qirkat, that had originally entered Spain from North Africa. Alquerque has two interesting features: it plays diagonally as well as horizontally and vertically, and a piece can capture an opponent by jumping over it—and can link multiple jumps together to capture several opponents in one turn.

Checkers ditches the horizontal and vertical moves and adds kings (or queens, depending on which country you're in) for pieces that reach the far end of the board. On reading the rules, you might think both games were similar, but, on playing, small changes make enormous differences. Players now have a reason to get their pieces to the other side of the board and the game has direction (two opposing directions, meeting in the middle). This creates different tactics, goals, and vibrant play.

The arrival of games made from a new material didn't erase the classic designs of stone and wood, but it was about to give them some stiff competition.

Left: Painted and inlaid wooden game board from late 17th-century India. This 8x8 side is for Chess or Checkers, while Backgammon can be played on the reverse.

CHECKERS • Year/period created: **1100CE** • Designer: **Unknown** • Place of origin: **Europe** • Number of players: **2** • Time to play: **30–120 minutes** • Complexity: **Low**

PAPER
AND PRINT

As paper became available in the 1400s, the nature of games changed, becoming more complex and flexible, more dynamic and transportable. They also developed into attractive, highly decorated items without having to involve hand-carved sets or inlaid boards. Plus their rules became standardized and recorded in rule books for posterity.

Right: The Game of the Goose, the first printed board game, moved quickly across Europe from Italy, printing in England in 1597. This French edition from 1890, *Grand Jeu de l'Oie* is held in Rambouillet, France, in the Game of the Goose Museum. **Above:** Cloisters playing card and detail from Game of the Goose.

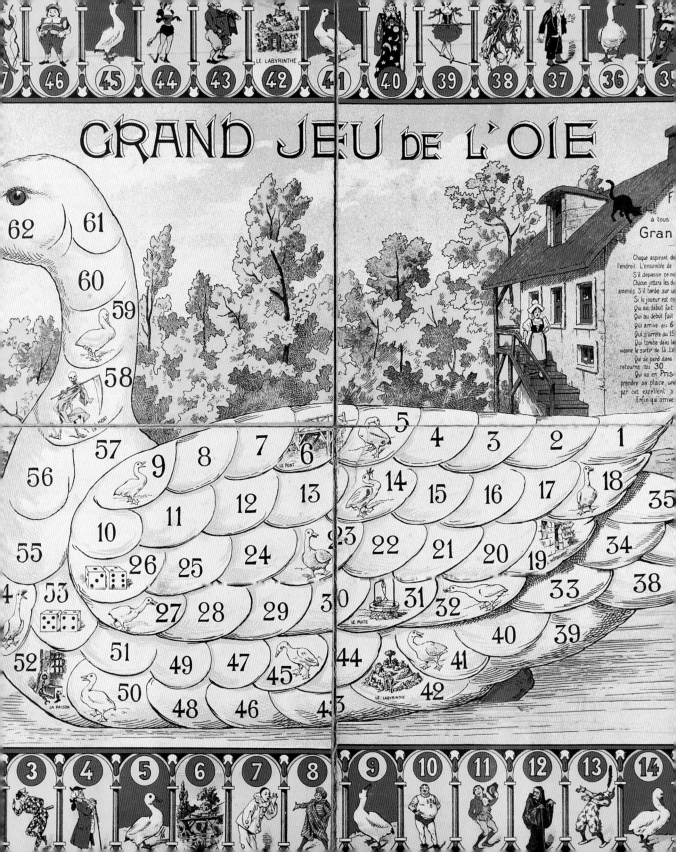

Reshuffling

It's impossible to cover the history of board games without mentioning playing cards. Though distinct from board games, they're an important part of the story.

The difficulty with cataloging the history of cards and other games made of paper or board is that they're delicate and more susceptible to the ravages of time than stone or wood. Like the cloth Pachisi boards in India, very few early cards have survived. We have loose descriptions of them and the games played with them but almost no actual examples.

Chinese card games

Playing cards and card games almost certainly first appeared in China, where their earliest reference dates to the Tang Dynasty (618–907CE) and something called *Yezi Ge* (the Leaf Game) in 868CE. More mentions follow over the next hundred years, but then the game died out. The word *yezi* went on to mean "playing cards," so it's tempting to say Yezi Ge was the first card game, but it's more likely to have been a gambling game played with dice or a drinking game with forfeits written on cards that were drawn randomly. Cards, yes, but not playing cards.

We do get a definite date a few centuries later for the existence of playing cards in China. On July 17, 1294, in Enzhou (modern-day Shandong Province), two men named Yen Sengzhu and Zheng Pig-Dog were arrested for playing cards, and the cards and the wooden blocks used to print them were impounded. Unfortunately, the Department of Punishments of the Yuan Secretariat was not concerned with recording

Cards from an original Chinese game

Main image: A selection of Visconti Sforza Tarot cards, dated to 1460–1470. Top row, left to right: The Empress, the Tower, the Devil. Bottom row: Death, the Wheel of Fortune, the Five of Coins. Behind: the Knight of Wands.

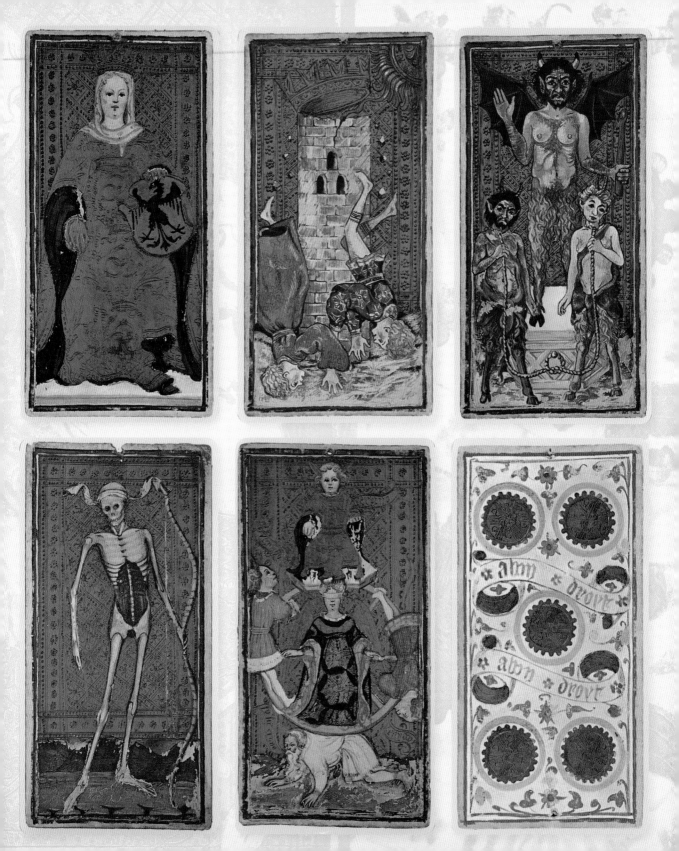

for posterity the design of the cards or the game that was being played. However, if having these cards was an arrestable offense, they were likely used for something nefarious, and where games are concerned, that usually means gambling.

The cards may have been "money cards"—decks based on Chinese currency, usually with four suits numbered from one to nine. Sir William Henry Wilkinson, the British Consul-General in China and Korea in the early 20th century and a keen playing-card collector, suggested that, since it was cumbersome to gamble with actual money, the Chinese may have used paper money instead and, over time, devised games to play with it. This could have also been a way of avoiding prosecution—though it didn't work for Sengzhu and Pig-Dog.

Left: Hand-drawn Mamluk cards from the 15th or early 16th century, each measuring 10x3¾in (252x95mm).

Following suit

Playing cards spread through India and Persia, and into Egypt. An almost-complete handmade deck of Egyptian Mamluk cards from around 1400 still exists, and there are fragments of even earlier ones in private collections. The Mamluk deck has 52 cards in four suits: swords, polo sticks, cups, and coins. Each suit is numbered from one to 10, plus has court cards known as *malik* (king), *naib malik* (deputy king), and *thani naib* (second deputy)—though these weren't picture cards yet. The Sunni Islam rules of the time forbade images of people in any form of art.

This set of cards probably sounds familiar, but why these four suits? It's possible that they represent four of the officers who attended a king or ruler: the sword-bearer, the polo master, the cupbearer, and the treasurer. Alternatively, the coins could be a holdover from Chinese money cards. But what's most interesting is the polo sticks. Polo is an ancient sport that originated in the Middle East and spread as far as Japan, but it was almost unknown west of Constantinople until the British Empire brought it to Europe in the 19th century. So when traders brought the first cards from Egypt to Italy and enterprising Italian gamblers began making their own decks, they would've had no idea what the polo-stick symbol was, so they changed it to wands or cudgels (a club-style weapon).

Cards are mentioned in southern Italian documents as early as 1365, and they spread across Europe like wildfire. At a time when information traveled no faster than someone on a horse, the cards made their way to Spain by 1371, Switzerland by 1377, Germany by 1378, and Paris by 1380. In almost every case, we know that they arrived in these places thanks to records of new laws banning certain new card games because of gambling.

The Italians translated the Egyptian symbols into coins, cups, swords, and wands. If you know Tarot cards, then you'll recognize these, but Tarot itself didn't emerge for another 80 years. In the Germanic countries, the four suits became leaves or shields, hearts or roses, bells, and acorns. As the game moved west to France, some of the Italian suits got mixed back in, becoming clover leaves, tiles, hearts, and pikes.

English suits are largely based on the French ones, with some confusion thrown in. Tiles became diamonds, and hearts remained hearts, but clubs and spades are blends of different influences. The word "clubs" originates from the name of the Italian staves or wands, but the suit's image is the French clover leaf. Similarly, "spade" is the Italian word for sword, though the symbol looks most like the German leaf design. The French symbols are considered to be the standard ones, and the French are also credited with dividing the deck into two red and two black suits.

Above: Mid-16th-century German woodcut of Italian preacher John Capistrano supervising burnings of gambling games and cards in the 1400s.

The four suits on playing cards were changed in different countries to fit local tastes.

Above: Selected cards from a complete set of South Netherlandish cards known as the Cloisters Playing Cards, dated to 1475–1480, more oval in shape than modern cards. The pictures are themed around hunting: the four suits are hunting horns, dog collars, hound tethers, and game nooses.

Initially, all playing cards would have been hand-painted, probably on commission for rich clients. The laws that forbade card play were not aimed at the upper classes but at the poor. Sometimes it took more than the threat of fines to stop people from playing. In 1452, Franciscan friar and Catholic priest John of Capistrano (1386–1456) preached so convincingly against the evils of gambling that the population of Nuremberg built a bonfire and burned 3,640 Backgammon boards, 40,000 dice, and an unspecified quantity of cards. History does not record who counted them all. However, despite the Church's best efforts, many cards survived, perhaps because they were attractive objects worth preserving, if not for playing with.

The earliest complete European deck is the Flemish Hunting Deck, also called the Cloisters Playing Cards, and you could play any modern card game with it. Fully painted and highlighted with gold, the cards date from around 1480 and are now in the Metropolitan Museum of Art in New York, which bought them from a Dutch collector in 1983 for $143,000 (now equivalent to $360,000). They show very few signs of wear. By 1480, painted cards were on the way out, now just a curio for the rich. For 60 years, German printers had been using woodblocks and engravings to print cards, coloring them by hand or with stencils. Some were extraordinarily beautiful.

The Carte da Trionfi spread from Italy and became known as Tarroco cards, then later as Tarock or Tarot.

TAROT CARDS (CARTE DA TRIONFI) • Year/period created: *Early 15th century* • Designer: *Unknown*

Place of origin: *Italy* • Number of players: *Varies by game* • Time to play: *Varies by game* • Complexity: *Varies by game*

Known only as the "Master of the Playing Cards," the greatest early printmaking artist created a five-suit deck of cards around 1450. In 2006, the Met bought a single one of his prints for $459,500.

"Queen of Flowers" card by the "Master," Germany, 1435–1440

Above: The Fool card painted for the Visconti-Sforza Tarot deck around 1460–1470.

The triumph of Tarot

Tarot cards, first known as Carte da Trionfi (Triumph Cards), emerged in the early 15th century in Italy. They began with a fairly standard deck of the Egyptian suits and four court cards instead of three (some decks of the time had up to six court cards). To this were added 21 new "triumphs" cards with allegorical illustrations that were used as trumps—special cards that could beat normal ones. We get the word "trump" from *trionfi*.

The earliest Tarot sets to survive are the Visconti-Sforza decks, from around 1460. Fifteen of these sets remain, though none is complete. Originally commissioned by Filippo Maria Visconti, the Duke of Milan, and his son-in-law Francesco Sforza, the cards are all hand-painted and include portrayals of the Visconti and Sforza families. The 21 trionfi cards are similar to today's Tarot decks, although most decks were not named or numbered at that time. The family may have been keen on creating so many decks because the Duke had apparently invented "a new and exquisite form of triumphs." His version, along with other trionfi games, has disappeared, though it was probably a trick-taking game—a sequence of turns where the highest card wins the hand, unless topped by a trump.

The Carte da Trionfi began to spread abroad in the 15th century, about the time of the Italian Wars. The war brought the cards to the French, who took to them in a big way, creating the 78-card Marseilles Tarot, which is the basis for almost all modern forms of the deck. Jeu de Tarot is the second-most popular card game in France today (after Belote). Outside mainland Europe, Tarot cards are best known for fortune-telling, but this association with the arcane didn't appear until the mid-19th century. In Continental Europe, games are still played with them, and cheap decks can be bought in newsstands and highway service station shops. Jeu de Tarot, also known as French Tarot, is a complex and tactical trick-taking game. Some cards, like the Fool, have special features, and there is a spare hand called the Dog. Scoring is complicated but worth the effort.

As the first printed cards began to roll off the presses in Germany, games were shifting toward a new and wider market. They were becoming visual, transportable, and affordable—in a word: commercial.

Wild Goose Chase

The introduction of the printing press in Europe changed board games, but not overnight.

In 1439, Johannes Gutenberg developed the movable-type printing press in Europe, revolutionizing the production and selling of books. This seismic change in communication had a profound effect on society, but it took a while for board games to catch up. Board games of the time had either a simple board and simple pieces that people could make themselves at home or a patterned board with carved pieces that required a craftsman or artist.

The first printed board game

We don't know who first came up with the idea of printing a game's board, or when they did, but we do know what and where. The game was called *Gioco dell'Oca*, or the Royal Game of the Goose, and it originated in Italy, probably in Florence. The earliest copies of the game that we have today are not very old, probably because the first paper boards did not survive. But there is mention of the game as far back as 1480 in a book of Italian sermons about the evils of playing dice games. We also know that the game spread across Europe, and the design of the board was registered at the Worshipful Company of Stationers in London by the English printer and bookseller John Wolfe in 1597. This registration was an early form of copyright law.

 Two surviving Game of the Goose boards can be seen today in the Metropolitan Museum of Art in New York. One originates from India,

John Wolfe registered the Game of the Goose as "the newe and most pleasant game of the Goose."

The Game of the Goose is a simple roll-and-move race to the center of a spiral course made up of 63 spaces.

Main image: This version of The Game of the Goose was printed, with woodcut and hand coloring, in the late 17th century. The printer's mark "In Venecia apresso/ Carlo Coriolani" can be found in the bottom-right corner.

THE ROYAL GAME OF THE GOOSE (*Gioco dell'Oca*) • Year/period created: *Before 1480* • Designer: *Unknown* • Place of origin: *Italy, possibly Florence* • Number of players: *2–6* • Time to play: *20–30 minutes* • Complexity: *Low*

the other from Morocco, and both are made from wood inlaid with ivory and metal. The Indian board dates from the 16th century, which has raised questions about whether the game is related to Mehen, an ancient Egyptian game also played on a spiral board. We can't be sure because, although Mehen boards have survived, the game's rules have not. Some people have also tried to connect the game to the Phaistos Disc. This is a Minoan artifact of unknown purpose with 241 symbols arranged in a spiral, which is at least 3,000 years old. However, apart from its spiral, it has no known link to the Royal Game of the Goose.

Above: This Indian board of ebony, ivory, and gold wire uses inlay techniques connected with the Gujarat area of India in the late 1500s. The reverse side holds a board for Chess and a non-European version of Backgammon.

One thing that is certain about the game (and possibly where the royal part of its name came from) is that around 1580, Francesco I de' Medici, Grand Duke of Tuscany, sent an ornate copy of it to Philip II of Spain. This is a charming parallel to the story about the origin of Chess and Backgammon (see p.42), and also the tale of the Dauphin of France sending a box of tennis balls to Henry V of England as a mocking response to his claim to the French throne. Francesco I's actions seem like curious diplomacy, particularly as he had a reputation as a playboy and Philip II was notably humorless, though perhaps that was the point. History does not record what Philip thought of the game.

The Royal Game of the Goose followed on the tails of Backgammon, Chess, and complicated trick-taking card games, but, to be blunt, it is a bad game. Every player places a stake (sometimes symbolic, sometimes money) in the center of the board, and the first to reach the middle claims it all. You roll two dice, move your piece, obey the conditions of the space you land on, and that's it. This game mechanic is as old as Senet and is one that people find endlessly pleasing, even though there is no skill to it.

Spiritual symbolism could be the reasoning behind certain icons appearing on specific numbered spaces: 63 was deemed the "grand climacteric" year of life and is the final square.

LUNA METE

Along the way to the winning spot are places like a bridge, a tavern, a well, a maze, and a prison, each with its own bonus or forfeit, such as missing a turn, moving to a different space, and paying more to the stake in the center of the board. The most common space on the board is a Goose, which lets you double your roll. However, the design of the game board is flawed: if your first throw is a 9, you move to 9, which is a Goose, so you move on another 9, to 18, which is also a Goose, as are 27, 36, 45, and 54. Landing on 63, the last space, wins the game, so you could win the game in your first turn, before anyone else has even had a chance to roll.

Modern designers would fix this game design by varying the positions of the Goose spaces, but our Florentine creator came up with a different solution—special spaces that you move to if you roll 3 and 6 (move to 26) or 4 and 5 (move to 53). It's not a great fix, since a player can still move to within 10 spaces of the end by rolling a 4 and a 5 as their opening throw. Games that lack strategy have to offer something else—such as tension and emotion—to keep players enthralled. As such, the end of the Game of the Goose holds more drama. The last space must be reached with an exact throw: rolling too high a number bounces your piece backward, possibly to land on space 58 (Death), which sends you all the way back to the starting point. In the even less-forgiving Spanish version, any throw that takes you past the final spot sends you straight back to the beginning of the board.

This page: An 18th-century woodcut Game of the Goose journeys from the Moon (Luna) to the Sun (Sole).

The Game of the Goose created the sense of going on an actual trip, in a way that previous abstract games had not been able to do. It was also the first to have a visible theme. The game set the template for simple race games that is still followed today: first-home-wins. The first to get home won half of the accumulated stake. The second and third to finish divided the rest

between them. So if you could avoid putting additional money into the middle, you could finish third and still come out ahead—except that's not actually something you could plan, because there can be no tactics in a completely random game. You can only obey the roll of the dice.

Why did such a simple game lacking in skill become so wildly popular across Europe? Possibly partly because it was unsophisticated: anyone could play, you couldn't be hustled by a better player, and remembering the different spaces provided a pleasing amount of thinking without ever making it feel hard. It may not be a good game by our standards, but nevertheless, it's satisfying to play.

The Royal Game of the Goose is the direct ancestor of modern race games, from the most basic to strategic ones like Formula Dé (a motor-racing game that has different-sized dice to simulate whichever gear the car is in). While it's historically interesting, as a game, it has aged badly indeed.

This page: In the 1800s, the race arena moved inside the body of the eponymous goose—now seen laying golden eggs. This engraving, on paper backed with linen and dated 1831, was printed by R. H. Laurie, potentially as a reproduction of an earlier version.

LAURIE'S NEW A...

ENTERTAINING GAME OF THE GOLDEN GOOSE.

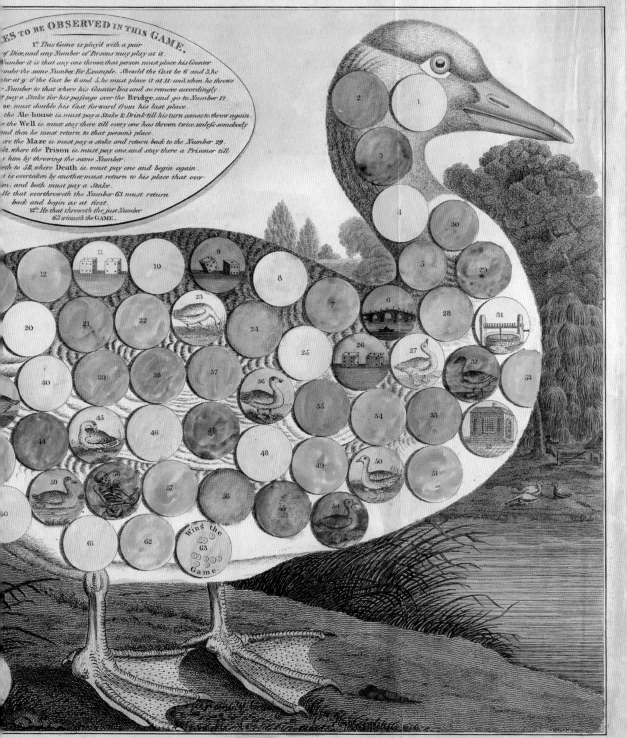

RULES TO BE OBSERVED IN THIS GAME.

1st This Game is play'd with a pair of Dice, and any Number of Persons may play at it.

...Number it is that any one throws, that person must place his Counter under the same Number. For Example. Should the Cast be 6 and 3, he ... at 9: if the Cast be 6 and 5, he must place it at 11: and, when he throws ... Number to that where his Counter lies and so remove accordingly ... pay a Stake for his passage over the Bridge, and go to Number 12 ... must double his Cast forward from his last place.

... the Ale-house is, must pay a Stake & Drink till his turn comes to throw again ... the Well is, must stay there till every one has thrown twice, unless somebody ... and then he must return to that person's place.

... the Maze is, must pay a stake and return back to the Number 29 ... where the Prison is, must pay one, and stay there a Prisoner till ... him by throwing the same Number.

... to 58, where Death is, must pay one and begin again.

... is overtaken by another, must return to his place that over... ... and both must pay a Stake.

... He that overthroweth the Number 63 must return back and begin as at first.

12th He that throweth the just Number 63 winneth the GAME.

Nov.r 22.nd 1846. by Richd. Holmes Laurie, No. 53, Fleet Street, London.

Above: This colored print from 1915/1916, France, used the game of Dominoes to teach children the flags of their country's allies during World War I. Individual pieces were designed to be cut out and then attached with a paper fastener. The rules of the game were printed in the center.

Domino tiles are part of the international Unicode Standard—a character coding system that holds scripts and symbol sets.

The mystery of Dominoes

After the arrival of the printing press, it's almost certain that people were taking the idea of the Game of the Goose and reworking it, but no evidence of these games remains. Unlike the Chinese, Indians, Persians, and Egyptians, European cultures have been lax about recording the games that they played. In the four centuries between the Alfonso *Libro de los Juegos* manuscript of 1283 and *De Ludis Orientalibus Libri Duo* by Sir Thomas Hyde in 1694, there were few books that we know of written about games in Europe.

What this means is that the origins of many games haven fallen through the cracks of history. Take Dominoes. Here is a hugely popular family of games, with sets available today in most toy and game stores. It's still played widely in China and the Caribbean. Yet its history is so obscure that the *Oxford History of Board Games* doesn't even mention it. The Chinese document *Former Events in Wulin*, written by Zhou Mi, states that peddlers sold dice and Dominoes in the 12th century. This is the earliest confirmed reference to Dominoes, but there is a theory that the "leaf game" (see p.56) mentioned in a Chinese text of 868CE may have been dominoes rather than early playing cards. A few Chinese authors mentioned them during the Middle Ages, and then sets appeared in Italy in the early 1700s.

These early Domino sets could have been brought to Europe from the east by returning traders. It has been speculated that Italian missionaries may have been responsible, but Dominoes uses the same pip patterns as dice, which many churches have long frowned upon because they are a tool for gambling, so perhaps not.

That's largely it for the known history of Dominoes. And if that's all the scholarship there is for such a well-known game, imagine how hard it is to find information about the 17th-century game *Il Laberinto dell'Ariosto* (Ariosto's Labyrinth), which is only known from two tantalizing mentions in two different books, published 120 years apart.

So, although we know that there were new games being created and played all over Europe, we know little about them. The next explosion of creativity in games would be in an educational context, 150 years later, and in a country that had so far shown little interest in the subject: Great Britain.

DOMINOES • Year/period created: **Possibly 12th century** • Designer: **Unknown** • Place of origin: **Possibly China** • Number of players: **2+** • Time to play: **Varies** • Complexity: **Low**

Amusing and Instructive

In the 150 years after the Game of the Goose swept Europe, something strange happened to games in the UK—new creations had the intention to be not only fun, but also educational.

These games of the late 18th and early 19th centuries were marketed as being educational but also as pleasant diversions and amusements. Their educational content is entirely passive—while players might absorb the dates of the kings and queens of Britain, or the primary industries of Northampton, the only thing they learn from the actual game play is that fate is random and victory or failure lies in the lap of the gods.

Geographical game play

A Journey Through Europe is the first game that tells us its creator (John Jefferys) and the date of its publication (1759). It's also the first game that is undoubtedly British and, for good measure, the first map-based game. It consisted of a large map of Europe printed on a single sheet of paper, cut into 16 rectangles, and glued to a sheet of canvas, meaning it could be folded without distorting the image. It was stored in a small slipcase, like the Carington Bowles maps that were the mainstay of Jefferys's business. The board measured 27x20 inches (69x52cm) and was tinted with

A Journey Through Europe cost 8s (the equivalent of £40, or $50, today), putting it out of the reach of all but the wealthiest.

Carington Bowles maps were often printed on 16 squares for easy folding.

Main image: The printed purpose of The Game of the Elephant and Castle, 1822, was "amusement with instruction for both sexes" on Asian customs, people, and events. It followed the first printed educational game: A Journey Through Europe or The Play of Geography, "Invented and sold by the Proprieter, John Jefferys, at his house in Chapel Street, near the Broad Way, Westmr. Writing Master, Accompt., Geographer, etc. Printed for Carrington Bowles, Map & Printseller, No 69 in St Paul's Church Yard, London. Price 8s. Published as the Act directs, September 14th, 1759."

watercolor paint. The map was then overlaid with the path of the game. A total of 77 numbered spaces lead from York in the north of England to Iceland, Scandinavia, Russia, and Ukraine, then west and south to Poland, Germany, Turkey, Greece, Italy, and across the Mediterranean for a very brief stop in North Africa, then north through Spain into France, across to Ireland, and finally back to England and the final stop in London. To the left was the key describing these places and the game effects of landing on them. Explanatory rules were printed on the right-hand side.

What exciting new game mechanics or innovations in game play had John Jefferys devised for his creation? "A Journey through Europe," declare the rules, "is to be played in all respects the same as the Game of the Goose." Clearly things had not changed much since 1597. There is some wit here— "He who rests at 48 at Rome for kissing ye Pope's Toe shall be banished for his folly to No [number] 4 in the cold island of Iceland and miss three turns"—and some clever ideas: "He who rests on any No where a King lives shall have ye priviledge [sic] to reckon his Spin twice over." This is the same mechanic as the geese in the Game of the Goose but fixed so that nobody can win the game with a single throw.

Most of the spaces have educational content rather than entertaining game effects, and many of them relate to Britain's glorious role in the world. However, such games were pricey and the rules very wordy, which in an age where education was a privilege meant that this was an item for the children of the rich, many of whom had a vested interest in Britain's prosperity and growing role as a global power.

Educational child's play

Jefferys did not appear to release any more games, but in the following decades, several other companies in London began producing games aimed at this juvenile market. Almost all of them were race games based on the Game of the Goose and played in a very similar way. There were minor variations: many of the games didn't use dice, because during this Victorian era, dice were seen as tools for gambling and consequently

A JOURNEY THROUGH EUROPE • Year/period created: *1759* • Designer: *John Jefferys*
Place of origin: *UK* • Number of players: *2–4* • Time to play: *60–90 minutes* • Complexity: *Low*

Published in 1741, John Wallis's "Arithmetical Pastime" aimed to "infuse the rudiments of arithmetic, under the idea of amusement".

An Arithmetical Pastime taught times tables and threatened repetitive forfeits for players who failed to correctly complete the sums.

Above: This original version of Wallis's Universal History and Chronology (1814) features Prince Regent George IV at its center.

The Game of Human Life ended on square 84.

Above: Every Man to His Station depicted five boys playing with 33 illustrated "walks of life"—from boatman and beggar to bishop and king.

GAME OF HUMAN LIFE • Year/period created: *1790* • Designer: *John Wallis and Elizabeth Newbery* • Place of origin: *UK* • Number of players: *2–4* • Time to play: *60–90 minutes* • Complexity: *Low*

had no place in good Christian homes. Instead, they were replaced with numbered spinners—teetotums—or a bag of numbered chits. Usually games involved a straight race, with no rules for variety, such as jumping other players' pieces.

The games fell into five types. The very first were literal reincarnations of the Game of the Goose. Then, following on from A Journey Through Europe, there were other geographical games, often based on maps, or combining maps and pictures. An exception in this category is The Noble Game of the Elephant and Castle, or Traveling in Asia (1822), which featured not a map but a series of numbered pictures on the side of a zoologically improbable elephant drawn by someone who had been nowhere near Asia, nor an elephant.

There was a wave of historical games, some tracing the line of English monarchs or the history of England, others like Wallis's New Game of Universal History and Chronology (1814), which begins with the Garden of Eden and ends with the current monarch. The game was often reprinted to reflect more recent events, such as the marriage of Queen Victoria.

Along with historical games came instructional games. These covered two different themes: educational subjects, such as An Arithmetical Pastime or Grammatical Game in Rhyme, and games of moral improvement, teaching right from wrong, good from bad, and living life well in the appointed fashion. Their (abridged) titles give a clue as to their content: Every Man to His Station (c.1825); The Reward of Merit (1801); Road to the Temple of Honour and Fame (1811); and The Swan of Elegance (1814).

For teaching human history, there's the Game of Human Life (1790), codesigned by map- and puzzle maker John Wallis and children's publisher Elizabeth Newbery. Players would begin on the first space, "The Infant," and move through the seven ages of man at the rate of one space a year, including Manhood (13–24), Old Age (49–60), and Dotage (73–84). Wallis and Newbery liberally borrowed from a French game, *Le Nouveau Jeu de La Vie Humaine*, released 10 years earlier. Life and how to live it is a theme that reappears throughout the modern history of games: Hasbro's The Game of Life is the best known today, but many others derive from this template.

THE COTTAGE OF CONTENT • Year/period created: *1848* • Designer: *William Spooner* • Place of origin: *UK* • Number of players: *Any number* • Time to play: *60–90 minutes* • Complexity: *Low*

Playing for fun

While the majority of surviving games from this era were educational, some were designed for pure amusement and fun, and departed from the track roll-and-move format. A Journey Through Europe and The Cottage of Content (opposite) are still races but hardly innovative in game design. Combat with the Giant (1796) used a deck of playing cards to act out an expedition to kill a fearsome monster, free its hostages, and share out the spoils of war. It was bizarrely complicated—even by modern standards—and featured more randomness than tactical choices, but it's one of the first games to pit players against a creature from myth. These games are highly collectible and expensive, not just because they're rare, but because their boards are beautifully covered in engraved pictures and coloured by hand.

Humans learn from playing games in two ways: passively, where they remember information that they have heard or read in the game (such as Trivial Pursuit, see p.140), and actively, learning by doing, where the player's moves, tactics, and interactions in the game teach them about the way the same process works in the real world—as in the original precursor to Monopoly (see p.76). The designers of the time almost certainly didn't intend these race games to be so passive, but the idea of learning through play was at its most nebulous. In 1794, German poet and philosopher Friedrich Schiller wrote an essay titled "Upon the Aesthetic Education of Man" in which he noted the importance of play and declared:

"Humans are only fully human when they play."

FRIEDRICH SCHILLER

No matter how poorly we perceive these games to have taught their subjects, the idea of learning through play was in the air. Innovators in areas such as women's rights and warfare would later pick up this theme. But first, games with increasing complexity would have to change again before they could take the next jump forward—they would need to be contained.

Many games of this era were deemed juvenilia and so weren't considered worth preserving at the time.

The Gaping, Wide-Mouthed, Waddling Frog (1823) is a reciting game in rhyme, published as a pamphlet, where a Dictator imposes forfeits on any who forget their lines.

In the 19th century, French priest Abbé Gaultier published a book of learning games to help him teach geography to children.

The aim of The Cottage of Content is for players to wind their way from the starting post to the eponymous cottage.

Left: The Cottage of Content (1848) is a morality game. Players must avoid penalties for taking the "wrong way," such as laughing at a man in the stocks or stealing a goose. The Cottage of Content allows players to decide their own path at a series of junctions by spinning a tee-otum marked forward, right, left, and back.

CARDBOARD

The 1800s invention of the cardboard box meant games with many parts could be easily transported and sold. This simple idea allowed game designers to create games with a greater number and variety of pieces than ever before, and that let them start to invent games with more complexity and diversity.

Right: With Monopoly, commercially released in 1935 but taken from Elizabeth Magie's earlier patented The Landlord's Game, games in cardboard packaging became a big, lucrative business.
Above: Panko cards and a Monopoly piece.

Play Fighting

The concept of storing games in boxes did not catch on right away, but the idea that games should have their own set of pieces was revolutionary. And in the early 1800s, Europe was in the grip of more than one revolution.

The very first commercial cardboard box was created in 1817, and it was used for The Game of Besieging, a strategic war game published in Germany. The box was not large by modern standards, not much bigger than this book, but it had enough room to contain the board, the rules, and 14 wooden pieces, carved and painted as stylized soldiers of red-and-blue armies. The game itself was an offshoot of the Tafl family (see p.48), but revamped with a modern theme. For game historians, the most interesting aspect to The Game of Besieging was its container. Finally, games had a format suited to their needs—and were easy to carry.

Portable war games

In 1812, George Leopold von Reisswitz presented Wilhelm III, the King of Prussia, with a copy of a game he had been developing. Reisswitz called it "Taktisches Kriegs-Spiel" (literally meaning "tactical war-game"). It was not the first war game, but anyone who knows modern war games will recognize many of its features, from the use of modular pieces to create the play surface, to rules that should have been made simpler.

The gift that arrived at the royal palace was not a cardboard box, but a wooden cabinet with a flat tabletop roughly 6½ sq ft (2 sq m).

Main image: The Game of Besieging, published in Germany c.1817-1820, an early stategy war game following rules established in preceding games. The hand-colored board could be folded to be transported in its accompanying cardboard box and came with 23 bone soldier playing pieces.

The board games of the 18th century came in pocket-sized wallets, with no space to contain pieces or teetotums.

A game in a box or other container meant that it could have its own specifically created set of components and these could be carried easily.

KRIEGSSPIEL • Year/period created: *1812* • Designer: **George Leopold von Reisswitz** • Place of origin: *Prussia* • Number of players: **2–8** • Time to play: *Unknown* • Complexity: *Medium*

Within the drawers of the cabinet were more than 300 plaster tiles, around 2½–4 sq in (7-10 sq cm), painted to show roads, villages, rivers, and other terrain, which could be arranged on the tabletop in many different configurations. There were also rectangular pieces representing troop types and equipment. Made of porcelain, these were painted different colors and inscribed with numbers and symbols. The cabinet also included dividers to measure distances, "small boxes for placing over certain areas so that troops who were unobserved might make surprise attacks," and most importantly, the rules—long, detailed, and filled with tables.

Military officers play the tabletop war game Kriegsspiel.

Von Reisswitz hadn't created his game from nothing. By the time he sent his invention to the king, Prussians had been developing war games for 150 years. These early games drew heavily on Chess. Christoph Weikhmann's *New-erfundenes Grosses-Königspiel* (Newly Invented Great Game of Kings) from 1664, for example, added eight new piece types corresponding to different types of military units, and reconfigured and expanded the checkered board into a network of circles connected by lines. The board for the two-player version of Weikhmann's game was the size of three regular chessboards, and the six-player version was a huge asterisk-shape, with six square boards connecting to a central hexagon. Although the game had some of the ideas and tactical diversity that constituted a war game, it was, essentially, a complicated version of Chess. Unlike similar games, there was no terrain, and the abilities of the pieces didn't bear any resemblance to the parts of the army they represented.

From Chess to Kriegsspiel

Many others tried to improve on the concept of Chess as a basis for a war game. German teacher Johann Christian Ludwig Hellwig's desire to teach military tactics to young men going off to serve in the armed forces led him to create his *Versuch eines aufs Schachspiel gebauten taktischen Spiels von zwey und mehrern Personen zu spielen* (1780), or "Attempt to build

Hellwig's original piece design sketches

German Prince Friedrich Ferdinand was a big fan of Hellwig's Das Kriegsspiel.

Christian Ludvig Hellwig was also an entomologist.

Hellwig didn't specify the size of his Kriegsspiel board. He suggested 49x33 squares (1,617 total) and sold boards at that size.

upon Chess a tactical game which two or more people might play." Starting with Chess, Hellwig expanded the board and introduced different-colored squares: white for ordinary ground, blue for water, red for mountains, and green for swamps. Suddenly, the board becomes a map.

Although Hellwig's pieces followed the moves of Chess pieces, in the first edition of his game, he gave them different strength values. These come into play for attacking fortifications: players were to add the combined strength of the attackers and compare it to the combined strength of the defenders. This was a new idea. Hellwig was full of new ideas. Two years later, he released an expansion for the game, which mostly clarified the rules, and in 1803, he published a complete second edition, shortening the name to Das Kriegsspiel: the Game of War.

By 1782, people were using the game to re-create actual battles, and the idea began to catch on in military circles. One of Hellwig's sets made its way to the young Prince Friedrich Ferdinand of Anhalt-Pless, who played it "constantly" against a friend—one George Leopold von Reisswitz. Von Reisswitz's "Taktisches Kriegs-Spiel" design owed an enormous amount to Hellwig's ideas. Von Reisswitz never completely finished the rules for his game; he left that to his son George Heinrich, who had fought in the Prussian Army against Napoleon's forces. The younger George worked with some of his fellow officers to produce a finished game, which he also called Kriegsspiel. Published in 1824, it set a template for military games and war games that is still recognizable today.

Among the younger von Reisswitz's key innovations was the addition of an umpire. In this revised version, the players of the two opposing armies (with up to four players on each side) could not talk directly to the other team but could communicate only through the umpire. They couldn't move their own pieces but were required to write down their orders—the umpires moved the units on the map and adjudicated on conflicts.

This transformed the game from a pleasant social exercise into something closer to a simulation. Later, different teams would be put in different rooms, unable to eavesdrop on each other's discussions and plans, while the umpire shuttled back and forth between them.

This new Kriegsspiel was well received. Von Reisswitz was asked to demonstrate it for Karl von Müffling, one of the heroes of Waterloo, who gave it a ringing endorsement. The game was taken up by the Prussian Army and all students of warfare, and von Reisswitz set up a factory to manufacture sets of the game—though these weren't aimed at the general public. For 30 thalers one could buy a set containing a paper map at 1:8,000 scale covering 4 sq miles (6.5 sq km), 26 battalions, 40 squadrons, 12 batteries, and one pontoon train, as well as dice, rulers and dividers, and a rule book.

The popularity of the game made von Reisswitz successful, but it also made him enemies who did not agree with the method of training he championed. In 1826, he was promoted to captain but given a new posting far from his friends and social circle in Berlin, which he saw as exile. Suffering from depression, he ended his life in September 1827.

Without its creator, the game was taken up by the first war-games club in the world, the Berliner Kriegsspiel-Verein. The club almost immediately issued a revised set of rules and helped ensure that Kriegsspiel was at the heart of Prussian military training for the next 40 years. After Prussia's final victory in the Franco-Prussian War in 1870, other countries took notice. Across Europe, war-gaming ideas and rules were borrowed from each other, where designs were refined to fit with national temperament and style of military training. Most of them used the original German name, Kriegsspiel, which became synonymous with this type of war game.

Marching into mass market

Some 100 years after Hellwig's original invention, two revisions brought Kriegsspiel to the wider public. One was Henry Temple's 1898 Chess variant with an umpire borrowed from Reisswitz. This featured three boards: the players each had a board with their own pieces on it, and the umpire had one that only they could see, with the pieces from both sides. The result was half Chess, half Battleship—players aimed to capture their opponent's pieces blind. It was decided it was more fun for the audience than for the players.

The other was the publication of the first commercial set of war game rules using miniature figures, bricks, toy forts, and volumes of the

In 1824, advertisements for Kriegsspiel appeared in the military newspaper *Militär-Wochenblatt* alongside Waterloo hero Karl von Müffling's endorsement.

Most versions of Kriegsspiel were published simply as a set of rules in book form.

Temple unhelpfully called his game Kriegspiel (with a single "s"), which has led to confusion ever since.

Wells used toy soldiers owned by his sons to construct his Little Wars.

Encyclopedia Britannica to build terrain to fight over. The book was *Little Wars*, and the game designer was H. G. Wells, author of *The War of the Worlds*, who roped in author friends such as Jerome K. Jerome to help.

Above: A feature in *Illustrated London News* (1913) shows H. G. Wells with his game of war. He is using string to measure his next move, curtains separate the two sides, and the umpire sits with a stopwatch.

H. G. Wells's *Little Wars* published by Frank Palmer, London, 1913.

The book is delightful, even though it is almost impossible to play *Little Wars* now as it was intended because the spring-loaded toy cannons the game required are no longer produced. Wells included an appendix on Kriegsspiel with his ideas for how to improve it, and why that might be a good thing: "Kriegspiel [sic], as it is played by the British Army, is a very dull and unsatisfactory exercise, lacking in realism, in stir and the unexpected, obsessed by the umpire at every turn, and of very doubtful value in waking up the imagination, which should be its chief function.... If Great War is to be played at all, the better it is played the more humanely it will be done. I see no inconsistency in deploring the practice while perfecting the method." *Little Wars* was published in 1913. A year later, a different Great War would be played out across Europe and beyond, and the public's thirst for war games would evaporate for some time.

LITTLE WARS • Year/period created: *1913* • Designer: *H.G. Wells* • Place of origin: *UK* • Number of players: *2–6* • Time to play: *Unspecified* • Complexity: *Medium*

CARDBOARD

Exit East

In the 1880s, a new fashion in Europe and the US for Asian objects and cultures had a profound impact on games and game design.

China and Japan were early game innovators, and their ideas and designs spread along the trade routes to India and the Middle East. They introduced such inventions as playing cards and tile-laying games like Dominoes. But in the 15th century, China's rulers made the conscious decision to cut the country off from foreign influence and closed its borders to traders and merchants. They declared to a British trade expedition in 1793 that "there is nothing we lack … nor do we want any more of your country's manufactures." Japan followed suit in 1639, expelling foreigners and closing its ports. It wasn't until after the first Opium War ended in 1842 that China reluctantly began to trade again with the West, including the UK and US. Japan did likewise within 20 years.

Reversing relations with the East

Even before China and Japan reopened their borders, there was much Western interest in Asia—if little accurate information about it. Early games such as An Eccentric Excursion to the Chinese Empire (1843) and The Elephant and Castle (see p.73) purported to be portraits of life there, but they were mostly based on rumor, caricature, and dubious sources.

It took a few years after trade was resumed for Eastern games to surface in the West, but Go (see p.20) was the first. Oskar Korschelt, a German chemist who had been working in Tokyo, wrote an article

Main image: A hand-drawn Sanskrit version of the Indian game Jnana Bagi (the Game of Heaven and Hell), a game now appropriated and better known in Western societies as Snakes and Ladders (or Chutes and Ladders).

A NEW WAVE OF GAMES FROM THE EAST

Reversi | Halma | Snakes and Ladders | Mahjong

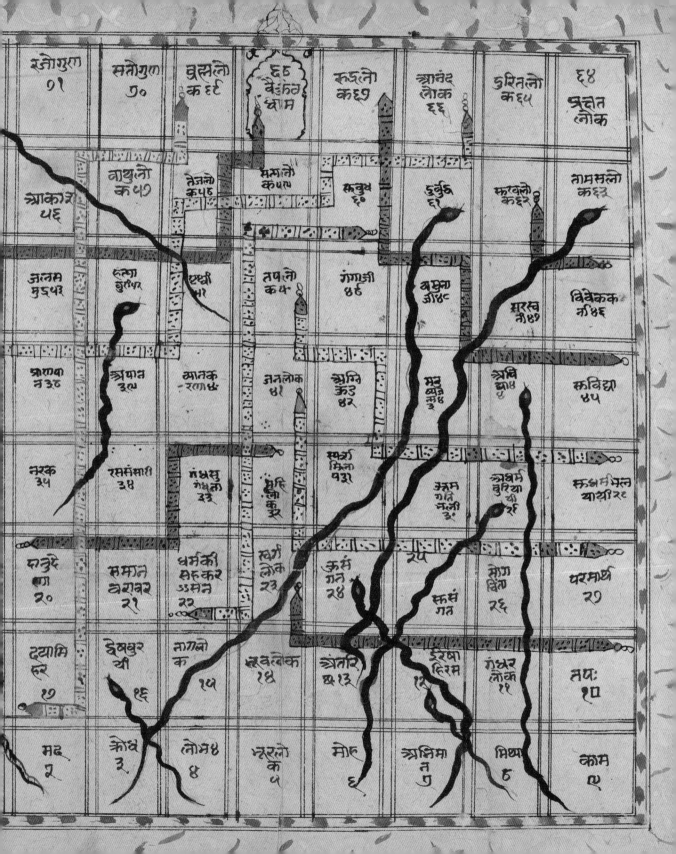

REVERSI • Year/period created: *Around 1885* • Designer: *Lewis Waterman or John W. Mollett*
Place of origin: *UK* • Number of players: *2* • Time to play: *Approx. 30 minutes* • Complexity: *Low*

about the game in 1883 and, a year later, a book.

European interest in Asian cultures was apparent in other aspects of society when one million people visited a reconstruction of a Japanese village in Kensington in London, and Gilbert and Sullivan's successful opera *The Mikado* opened in 1885. And with these ersatz imports came a debased form of Go, known in Japan as Gomoku and in Britain as Go Bang. Gomoku isn't Go, but it does use the same board and stones. Players take turns to place a stone, and the winner is whoever completes a straight line of five of their color first. (Gomoku is often known as Five in a Row.) Imagine a more strategic version of Tic-Tac-Toe on a bigger board or of Connect Four without the gravity.

Around the same time as Gomoku appeared, Reversi was invented by either Lewis Waterman or John W. Mollett; both Englishmen claim the honor. Reversi is an abstract game of territory control played on an 8x8 grid with tiles that are white on one side and black on the other. It looks very much like the kind of game that might be invented by someone who has seen pictures of Go but had no explanation of the rules.

To win Reversi, you need to be the player with the most tiles of your color on the gridded board. On your turn, you place a tile, your color up, so that at least one of your opponent's tiles are trapped between your new one and one you'd already placed. All the trapped tiles are then flipped over to become your tiles. It plays much faster than Go, and its strategies are more obvious, but it's an engrossing and entertaining game. It was invented again in 1968, back in Japan, and marketed under the name it's usually known as by today: Othello. Reversi isn't a true Japanese game, more a European idea of what a Japanese game might be—just like other modern-day games such as Takenoko, Tokaido, and Sushi Go.

Wooden Reversi packaging from the 1920s.

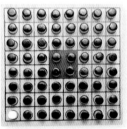

Above: Reversi with tall pegs in holes rather than tiles on a flat board.

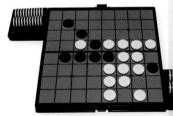

Above: Modern Othello with a green-felt topped board. World Othello Championships have been held every year since 1977.

Not-Chinese Chequers

Another game with more than a passing resemblance to Go is Halma, invented in the US in the 1880s. In Halma, the aim is to move all your pieces from one corner of a square board to the other, while your opponent moves theirs in the opposite direction. In the four-player version, two additional players take the other two corners of the square.

Above: George Howard Monks, who also invented Basilinda—a war game of sorts involving cannons, captains, and king pieces.

In some versions of Halma, six players can play around the star. Each takes a point of the star as their own and attempts to transfer their pegs to the opposite point.

Left: Illustration of a family enjoying the four-player version of Halma on a square board.

The swapping-ends idea comes from Backgammon, and the movement that lets you hop opponents' pieces is taken from Checkers (or Draughts)—though the hopped pieces stay where they are instead of being taken away. Halma's inventor was George Howard Monks, a thoracic surgeon from Harvard, who was inspired by an 1854 British game called Hoppity.

Halma became successful enough for the German company Ravensburger to publish a six-player version on a star-shaped board in 1892 called Stern Halma (Star Halma). The fledgling American company Pressman spotted it in 1928 and made its own version, which it called Hop Ching Chequers and later renamed Chinese Chequers. It's not Chinese, and it's not Checkers, but it is still widely played today, and you'll find it in many boxes of classic board games.

Left: American 1930s version of "Chinese Checquers." The box has an artistic impression of a Chinese temple, and the star is cornered by dragons. Pegs are stored down the side of the box.

HALMA • Year/period created: **c.1880** • Designer: **George Howard Monks** • Place of origin: **US** • Number of players: **2, 4, or 6** • Time to play: **Approx. 30 minutes** • Complexity: **Low**

SNAKES AND LADDERS • Year/period created: *Modern version: 1892* • Designer: *Unknown*

Place of origin: *UK* • Number of players: **2 or more** • Time to play: *Up to 45 minutes* • Complexity: *Low*

Simplifying Snakes and Ladders

In 1892, Snakes and Ladders appeared in the UK. It was a dumbed-down version of a family of Indian games with very ancient roots, which instructed players on morality and spirituality. Gyan Chaupar or Moksha Patam may date back as far as the 2nd century BCE. Players rolled dice to progress across a board of numbered squares as well as through the layers of understanding embodied in Hindu or Jain beliefs: liberating the soul from earthly desires, increasing devotionalism, and reaching spiritual enlightenment. But they must beware, lest they slip back towards the bottom by following various vices, shown as snakes. Mokshapat (Heaven and Hell) from the 13th century continued this idea of rewarding virtue with ladders and punishing vice with snakes. Jnana Bagi, from the 18th century, has 82 squares full of symbolism. The longest ladder carries virtuous players from number 17, marked "compassionate love," to number 69, labeled "the world of the absolute."

The new British game lost all this spiritual significance. Instead it focused just on simple moral tales with little improving illustrations: at the top of a snake, a child eating an entire cake would be seen suffering the consequences at the bottom. Over time, even these simple lessons were removed, leaving just the ladders and snakes. The game is pure luck, dependent on dice rolling: the only decision the player can make is whether to kick the board over and play something better. Despite this, it's very well known in the UK, and almost everyone has played it. But for the rest of the world, even its original homeland, it's just another game.

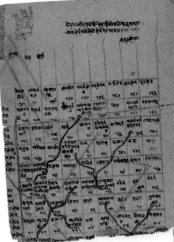

Parchment fragment of an Indian Snakes and Ladders

Mokshapat was invented by the Indian saint Gyandev in the 13th century.

In the US, Snakes and Ladders is mostly known through the 1943 defanged MB Games version called Chutes and Ladders.

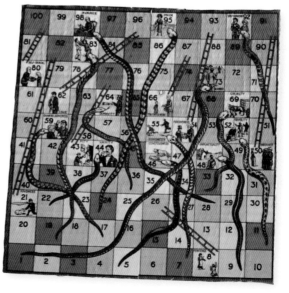

Right: This Eurocentric Edwardian version of Snakes and Ladders from 1905 features morality-themed squares, such as vanity, unpunctuality, pride, avarice, and frivolity— all of which lead to a serpentine tumble.

The basics of Mahjong are always the same, but there are many regional variations of the rules and scoring.

A full set of 144 Mahjong tiles. Three dice are used to determine who plays first.

Maintaining Mahjong's identity

About the only Asian import to survive the journey from its homeland without significant change was Mahjong. The game isn't particularly old compared to many other games from China; it probably evolved from other games. The earliest surviving sets date from around 1870.

Mahjong's popularity spread gradually across its home country until it reached the ports along the coast, where it was taken first to America and then probably from there to Europe. As in China, its progress was slow at first, and it took off only in the 1920s when Abercrombie & Fitch decided to retail it. Initially, Americans used a streamlined set of rules known as The Red Book, but they soon discarded that and went back to the original.

Mahjong is effectively a card game played with tiles. A set has 144 tiles, comprised of three suits of Simples, two sets of Honors (winds and dragons), and two sets of Bonus tiles (flowers and seasons). Players make sets of these to create a winning hand of 14 tiles.

Mahjong is a game that delights both the intellect and the senses, with the feel of the tiles and the sound they make as they're pushed together combining to create a unique experience.

MAHJONG • Year/period created: **Around 1850** • Designer: **Unknown** • Place of origin: **China** • Number of players: **3 or 4** • Time to play: **Varies** • Complexity: **High**

TURN 'EM OUT!

(Copyright.)

VOTES FOR WOMEN

CARDBOARD

Campaign Games

In the 1900s, the battle lines are drawn—
on and off the board.

On one end of a street stands a line of green-clad Suffragettes, activists demanding votes for women, intent on getting into the Houses of Parliament. On the other end stand the police in blue, seeking to block the Suffragettes and disrupt their meeting at the Albert Hall. Political agenda has started to infiltrate gaming in a big way—from the French Revolution, to women's suffrage, to World War II and beyond.

Votes for Women!

It was the height of the women's fight for equality in the United Kingdom, and the Women's Social and Political Union (WSPU), founded in 1903, had grown tired of the pacifist tactics of its sister organizations. Its founders, mother and daughter Emmeline and Christobel Pankhurst, took the more militant approach of holding rallies and marches, smashing windows, disrupting events, and, when they were inevitably arrested, going on hunger strike. Running a political campaign takes money, and the WSPU was initially reliant on donations from its middle-class supporters. Desperate to be more independent, one of its many marketing ideas was to publish games to draw both attention and revenue to the movement. The first was probably The Game of Suffragette, produced in 1907 by the Kensington branch of the organization: a card game with 54 cards divided into 13 suits with names such as "Freewomen," "Prominent Supporters," and "Arguments."

Ironically, the Suffragetto game instructions use "he" and "him" to refer to players.

PANK! PANK! PANK!

Main image: Pank-A-Squith spiral race board distributed and sold by the Women's Social and Political Union, first advertised in 1909. The central goal is to reach the Houses of Parliament, passing squares featuring topical figures and locations such as Emmeline Pankhurst, Prime Minister Herbert Asquith, Trafalgar Square, and Holloway Prison. *Additional images:* Two Panko cards.

SUFFRAGETTO • Year/period created: *1908* • Designer: **Women's Social and Political Union (WSPU)** • Place of origin: **UK** • Number of players: **2** • Time to play: *30 minutes* • Complexity: Low

Players had to collect sets of cards relating to the struggle, each worth a certain number of points. The cards carried photographs of notable Suffragettes and trivia questions about the cause.

The Game of Suffragette was successful enough to inspire other games, and the most interesting—both as a game and a political antique—is Suffragetto (origins unclear, but believed by many to be by the WSPU), a board game of a clash between evenly balanced forces of Suffragettes and police. The Suffragette player must get six pieces into the Houses of Parliament, the police player must also get six pieces into the Albert Hall, and the two sides clash in an area known as the Arena, totaling 9x17 squares. In reality, of course, the two are 2.5 miles (4km) apart!

This is not a war game in the Kriegsspiel (see p.78) sense. The rules are simple and printed on a single sheet of paper. The pieces consist of two sets of large and small pawns that can hop over each other. If that hopping happens in the Arena, then the opposing piece—if a Suffragette—is moved to the Prison or—if a police person—to the Hospital. In play, it sits between Checkers and Hnefatafl (see p.48) and is fun enough for several games.

Of course, it's what Suffragetto represents that makes it interesting. Games and game players had learned the lessons of the 18th and 19th centuries: games can be used to teach factual information, to inform, and to create tactics and strategic thinking in their players, along with an understanding of processes and systems. Suffragetto and its sister games were the forerunners of a third purpose for games: spreading a political or philosophical message. The moral games of the London publishers had made the first moves in this direction, but this was propaganda, eagerly bought by the movement's supporters and subverted by its opponents.

No sales figures for Suffragetto exist, but these games were popular enough for the WSPU to release further games the year after: Panko and

Pank-A-Squith game board

Panko and Suffragettes In and Out of Prison instruction pamphlets

LAW! LAW! LAW!

(Copyright.)

VOTES FOR WOMEN.

(Copyright.)

GAOL! GAOL! GAOL!

(Copyright.)

The Panko card game features Suffragist suits in symbolic mauve and green and anti-Suffragists in red and black.

Pank-A-Squith, taking their names from the founders of the movement (the latter combined with PM Herbert Asquith). Sadly, Suffragetto did not survive the era, and only one original copy is known today, in the Bodlean Library in Oxford.

These examples show how games were used to convey political or campaigning messages, or as reactions to the news of the time. They had become just another part of the boom in mass media. Advances in printing allowed intricate designs with color art or photographs to be published quickly and cheaply.

Produced at the same time, Suffragettes In and Out of Prison was not raising funds for any movement, but was a commercial game attempting satire priced at one penny (about twice the price of a newspaper), published by *The Morning Leader* in 1908. A single sheet of card with a cheaply printed spiral roll-and-move game on it, players had to get from the center of the spiral (Holloway Gaol) to the outside, avoiding policemen, walls, and the wardress. One surviving version was bought from a trader outside St. Paul's Cathedral, where copies of A Journey Through Europe had been sold 150 years earlier.

Vive la Révolution!

On the other side of the Channel, the French had been making political games for years. The *Jeu de la Révolution Française* was published in France in 1791, telling the history of the revolution that had begun two years earlier. As a game, it's the Game of the Goose (see p.46) all over again, right down to the 63 squares and a death on square 58—in this case, the beheading of the politician Foulon. As a playable chronicle of unfolding events, it could be one of the first interactive history lessons.

Then from the late 19th century, there is the Siege of Paris, played on a checkerboard with a fort in the middle. Besiegers outnumber defenders and, to win, must occupy the fort with at least one officer and three soldiers. But this presumably isn't a French game, since the box and the rules are in English. The same is true of A New Game of Russia versus Turkey, from 1853, inspired by the early naval engagements of the Crimean War.

FOURTEEN DAYS!

(Copyright.)

HELP! HELP! HELP!

HELP! HELP! HELP!

(Copyright.)

Panko cards

JEU DE LA RÉVOLUTION FRANÇAISE • Year/period created: *1791* • Designer: *Unknown*

Place of origin: *France* • Number of players: *2–4* • Time to play: *60 minutes* • Complexity: *Medium*

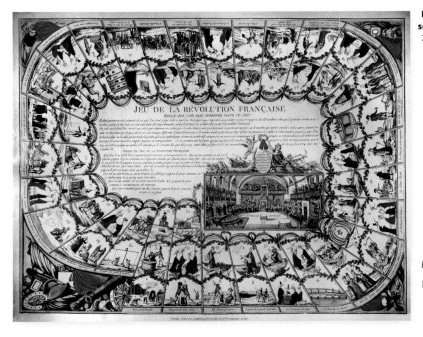

Details of squares 62, 32, and 2.

Left: The *Jeu de la Révolution Française*, where players can witness events of the French Revolution unfold over 63 squares.

Half a century later, Called to Arms is a simple race game based on the Boer War, first published in c.1900 while the war was still in progress. Although the most prominent flag on the board is British and the game is filled with patriotic fervor, the only known copies were published in Australia. The country was still part of the British Empire, and around 16,000 Australians fought in the war, although it's unlikely they would have recognized their experiences from this sanitized version of events.

In *Jeu de la Révolution Française,* each square depicts a scene, from the storming of the Bastille (square 1) to the formation of the National Assembly (63).

World War II and beyond

Propaganda, of course, goes both ways. The ugliest example of a game based on real-world events is *Juden Raus!* (Jews Out!), published in Germany in 1938. It wasn't produced by the Nazis, but like Suffragettes In and Out of Prison, it looks like a commercial attempt to profit from the wave of public feeling whipped up by anti-Jewish laws and propaganda. The theme is so reprehensible that even *Das Schwarze Corps,* the newspaper of the SS, criticized the game for trivializing its subject. *Juden Raus!* appears to have sold very badly, and only a handful of copies survived the war, most of them now in museums.

During World War I, *The Strand Magazine* produced a game where Allies were pitched against German forces in a version of Draughts/Halma.

Wir Fahren Gegen Engeland box

Bomber Command (2012 reissue)

Bomber Command requires each player to fly four bomber planes to Berlin and back.

The game Blackout was produced in the US two years before the country's involvement in World War II.

The Nazis did sanction other games in this era, from designs as simple as a Pachisi board in the shape of a swastika, to *Wir Fahren Gegen Engeland* (We are Driving Against England) in 1942, which puts players in control of submarines sinking ships off the coast of Britain. In *Jagd auf Kohlenklau* (Hunt on Coal Theft), a spiral roll-and-move game from c.1944, family members were encouraged to save energy and punished for wasting it.

The UK and the US produced their share of propagandistic games based on the war effort, too. Bomber Command (from the 1940s) was a simple roll-and-move game about bombing Berlin, with dice that had to be constructed out of thin card; in Decorate Goering, players were encouraged to pin medals on the Reichstag president tail-on-the-donkey style; and in Blackout, produced by MB Games in America in 1939, players had to block out all the light from their bright cities.

The strangest and most effective use of a board game during the war involved a game that had nothing to do with warfare. During World War II, some relief packages sent to British prisoners of war in camps in Axis territory contained copies of the then 10-year-old game Monopoly, the American design produced under license in the UK by John Waddington Ltd. However, these editions had actually been designed by Christopher Hutton of MI9, a division of British Intelligence created for "escape and evasion." They contained silk "escape" maps hidden in shallow compartments inside the boards (silk is thin, light, and durable, and makes no sound when folded), along with a compass, small tools, German currency hidden among the paper money, and playing pieces made of gold covered in a thin layer of lead. Waddington was a willing accomplice in this subterfuge and pioneered the techniques needed to print on silk.

Sadly, none of these special games survived, but it's estimated that almost 750 British troops escaped with the help of Waddington's maps, which were also concealed in decks of cards, Chess sets, and copies of Snakes and Ladders. Never has the "Get out of jail free" card been so apt.

ESCAPE AND EVASION MONOPOLY • Year/period created: *1947* • Designer: *Christopher Hutton* • Place of origin: *UK* • Number of players: *2–4* • Time to play: *60–90 minutes* • Complexity: *Medium*

Monopolies and Mergers

Who are the creators behind many of the popular board games to come out of the 19th and 20th centuries?

Many of the first game publishers in the 1700s had been map makers or educational publishers. Few of the first small games makers survived more than a generation, but with a new wave of games, new foreign designs to borrow or occasionally license, and cardboard boxes to make attractive packages, entrepreneurs saw an opportunity to go further.

Bradley's borrowed Game of Life

Milton Bradley is the oldest of the modern game companies. Bradley himself was a lithographer, his biggest seller a portrait of Abraham Lincoln. When Lincoln grew a beard, making Bradley's stock unsellable, he was inspired by an imported board game given to him by a friend, George Tapley, and in 1860 designed and produced The Checkered Game of Life. He sold the first printing in two days in New York and, by the end of the year, had sold more than 40,000 copies.

The Checkered Game of Life is clearly based on earlier English and American games of fortune such as The New Game of Human Life (1790) and The Mansion of Happiness (1800), which had been republished in the US in 1843. But Bradley's game emphasizes success in the world over the earlier games' goals of virtue and spiritual attainment—squares that score highly include college, wealth, congress, and happy old age.

The Checkered Game of Life does not feature dice, since these were associated with gambling.

Still in print today, The Game of Life sees players choose their dream career and move along a track.

__Main image:__ Elizabeth Magie's patent for The Landlord's Game from 1903, and Monopoly, which preceded it. __Additional images:__ Milton Bradley, inventor of The Checkered Game of Life.

THE GAME OF LIFE • Year/period created: *1860* • Designer: *Milton Bradley* • Place of origin: *US*
Number of players: *2-4* • Time to play: *60-90 minutes* • Complexity: *Medium*

It also has negative squares, including gambling, poverty, ruin, and suicide.

The Checkered Game of Life is a point-scoring game rather than a race—it's laid out on a checkerboard, and the spin of a teetotum tells the player which direction to move; squares may give you points or direct you to other squares. The first to 100 points wins.

Milton Bradley Games became MB Games and published hundreds of games, including iconic classics like Candyland, Chutes and Ladders, and Twister.

Milton Bradley's The Checkered Game of Life

Meanwhile, Tapley, who had given Bradley the game that inspired him in the first place, became director of the company in the late 1870s.

Trading games and names

At just 16, schoolboy George S. Parker created his first game in 1883. Reflecting the monetarist mood of the time, it was called Banking and was a game of speculation using 160 lettered cards. George speculated $40 of his own money to print 500 copies and sold all but 12 of them. Still at school in Massachusetts, he set up a company named after himself—it would become Parker Brothers when his brother Charles joined in 1888—and released four more titles in two years, including Ivanhoe and The Dickens Game, neither with any permission from the authors whose works appeared in them.

On the other side of the Atlantic, J. W. Spear & Sons (considered one of the great brands for British board games) was founded in 1879 as a joint Anglo-German operation by Jacob Wolf Spear—who had changed his name from Spier—and two of his sons. Its toys and games were made in Germany, in a factory outside Nuremburg, and mostly exported to the UK. In 1932, the company moved its manufacturing to north London, partly to escape the rise of the Nazis and partly to avoid customs duties.

In The Checkered Game of Life, the ambition square leads to fame, whereas crime leads to prison.

Ravensburger is still run by the family of its founder, the Maiers. Milton Bradley Games, Parker Brothers, and Waddingtons are all part of Hasbro Inc. today. J. W. Spear & Sons (Spear's Games) was taken over by Mattel in 1994.

Meanwhile, the German factory was handed over to supporters of the Nazis, and it continued to publish games including *Bomben Auf England*. The Spear's Games factory went on to publish classics such as Scrabble (1953), Coppit (1964), and Othello (1971).

Spear's Games wasn't the first success in the German game industry. The same year that Parker Brothers released Banking, Ravensburger was founded by Otto Robert Maier in the German town of Ravensburg. At first, it produced plans for architects and craftsmen, but later released its first game, Journey Around the World. It's now known for Labyrinth, Enchanted Forest, Scotland Yard, and for winning the Spiel des Jahres—the prestigious global games prize—more times than any other company.

John Waddington began business as a Yorkshire-based printer for the theater industry before moving into games in the early 1900s.

Pit's Edgar Cayce went on to become a famous psychic!

Left: Edgar Cayce's Pit from 1904 is a shouting stock-trading game where the player who corners the market in a commodity wins. The first with a full set rings the bell and brings trading to a close.

Pratt gained inspiration for Cluedo (originally named Murder!) from his time spent performing music in country hotels where murder-mystery games were part of the evening's entertainment.

Many of its games were licensed from Parker Brothers in the US, notably Pit and Monopoly and, later, Risk. The Americans snapped up the US rights to Cluedo (Clue) after Waddington acquired the game from its inventor, Anthony Pratt, copyrighting it in 1949, and produced a US edition of the 1930s pirate game Buccaneer, which was marketed as Trade Winds.

There is one other notable game company that has survived from the 19th century, though it has changed beyond all recognition. The Nintendo Playing Card Company was founded in 1889 by Fusajiro Yamauchi. After dabbling in businesses such as taxis and love hotels, it expanded into toys in 1966, electronic toys in 1973, handheld LCD video games in 1979, and the Famicom (Family Computer) video game system, known outside Japan as the Nintendo Entertainment System, in 1983. It came bundled with the game Super Mario Bros and introduced the character who changed the face of video games forever. Nintendo still manufactures playing cards in Japan and organizes a contract bridge tournament called the Nintendo Cup. If video games ever collapse, at least it'll have something to fall back on.

Elizabeth Magie's The Landlord's Game

As the business of games became more businesslike, the subject matter of many games steered toward commerce, money, trading, and the stock market. Parker Brothers' Banking was only the first of its games about monetary success. It is a great irony that the most financially successful board game of the 20th century started life as a damning criticism of capitalism and financial greed. It's a story of theft, deceit, and trickery and, like the game itself, doesn't have much of a happy ending for its creator. If you hadn't guessed, the game is Monopoly, and its inventor was Elizabeth Magie, born in Illinois in 1866. Not only has her part in the history been almost lost but so has the true purpose of this game.

The Landlord's Game, Magie's creation, is one of the first games to have mechanics and play that specifically demonstrate the game's central theme—that the system of buying and renting property will lead to greater wealth for the rich and poverty for everyone else. Magie was an unorthodox woman who earned her living as a stenographer (shorthand typist), wrote poetry, performed comedy roles on stage, and designed games. Magie was also a follower of the economist Henry George and saw games as a way to demonstrate Georgist theories of how money changed hands in the property market.

Originally The Landlord's Game came with two sets of rules: one in which everyone gained when profits were created, and a second that showed the iniquities and greed of the monopoly system.

The Landlord's Game is an early example of a continuous-path game—almost all games before it had clear start and end points.

The concepts of Easy Money and Finance were based on The Landlord's Game.

Chance cards in The Landlord's Game carried quotes from philosophers and economists.

No. 748,626.

PATENTED JAN. 5, 1904.

L. J. MAGIE.
GAME BOARD.
APPLICATION FILED MAR. 23, 1903.

NO MODEL.

2 SHEETS—SHEET 1.

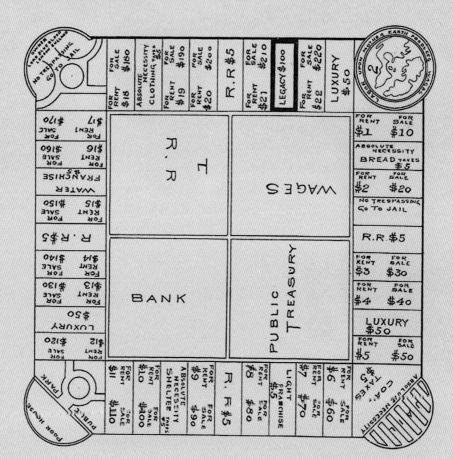

Fig. 1.

Witnesses
F. L. Ourand.
M. H. Ourand.

Inventor
Lizzie J. Magie
by John A. Saul
Attorney

Magie devised and patented The Landlord's Game in 1903 and published it through her own business, the Economic Game Company, in 1906, selling copies around the northeast of the US with limited success. In 1909, Magie offered The Landlord's Game to Parker Brothers. It was rejected, but by then the game was catching on, and players were making their own versions, changing the board's design, localizing it to include familar street names, and tweaking some of the rules. But crucially, they also gave it different names: Finance; Auction; and Monopoly.

It was one of these ersatz versions that was spotted by Charles Darrow, a domestic heater salesman. He designed his own version and began producing copies for sale around Philadelphia, patenting it in 1933. He also showed his version to Parker Brothers, who initially rejected it for being too complex, but after seeing how well it was selling, they changed their minds and published it in 1935. Parker Brothers credited Darrow as the sole inventor, but only after buying Magie's remaining patents on The Landlord's Game without telling her about Darrow's version, or their plans. Within a year, it was selling 20,000 copies a week. Other companies rushed to imitate its success: Milton Bradley's Easy Money (1935) is clearly based on The Landlord's Game.

Monopoly helped make Charles Darrow become a millionaire, but his other game, Bulls and Bears (1936), was not a success.

Magie created several more games and sold other designs to Parker Brothers, but The Landlord's Game was her greatest success, albeit in a version that didn't bear her name, paid her very little, and celebrates greed and ruthless capitalism instead of critiquing it. Original copies of The Landlord's Game are among the rarest games of the 20th century and have sold for more than $50,000. Magie would probably not have approved.

Left: Prize-winning box from British Monopoly Championship 1975. **Right:** Metal Monopoly pieces: top hat, train, thimble, boot, car, and dog.

MONOPOLY • Year/period created: *1935* • Designer: **Charles Darrow** • Place of origin: *US* • Number of players: **2–6** • Time to play: **60–240 minutes** • Complexity: *Medium*

Above: Modern American Monopoly board. Similarities between The Landlord's Game and Monopoly include: the use of real place names; Chance squares; the Jail and Go To Jail squares; and the Go! square that was originally marked Labor Upon Mother Earth Produces Wages.

PLASTIC

The first plastics appeared in games at the end of the 19th century in the form of dice and counters. The material's mass production in the 20th century, combined with game designers and manufacturers beginning to understand the potential of plastic, meant the shape and scope of the games being created changed completely.

Right: The introduction of plastic meant that games such as Risk could have boxes filled with plastic soldiers, tanks, and planes instead of cardboard chits or wooden blocks.
Above: Scrabble tiles and a pair of dice.

Batteries Not Included

Plastic changed everything, but in games its effect was first felt at the junior end of the market.

The 1950s and 1960s produced a long succession of brightly colored games. These were often accompanied by heavy advertising and negligible game play, to be abandoned by players in a few hours and by the publishers in a few months. But these decades also spawned a share of classics, some from major companies that were switching from war work back to light entertainment, and others from independent designers.

Spelling a success for Scrabble

Then, as now, companies either designed games in-house, were pitched to by creatives with clever ideas, or purchased the rights to existing games or the companies that produced them. Sometimes it was a mixture of all three. Scrabble is one of the great almost-misses of game history—a game that nearly failed twice. Although it became a smash hit in the mid-1950s, it had a rocky start. Unemployed architect Alfred Butts invented the game, which he called Lexiko, in New York at the height of the Great Depression in 1933. Players drew wooden letter tiles and tried to make seven-letter words from them. After publishers weren't interested, Butts released it himself, making the sets on his kitchen table. He sold fewer than 100 in the first year.

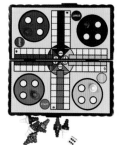

The use of plastic turned Ludo into the colorful, pop-o-matic game known as Frustration in the UK and Trouble in the US.

Main image: Royal Ludo from 1900s. The use of plastic transformed this game, and produced games that could not have been made otherwise, such as Kerplunk and Mouse Trap. It wasn't a cheap or quick process, but it made games with special pieces easier to manufacture and more affordable to buy.

Left: Spear's Games' Scrabble as produced in the UK in 1954, with green cardboard box and plastic tiles. The letters are given different values in different languages.

SCRABBLE • Year/period created: *1933* • Designer: *Alferd Butts* • Place of origin: *US* • Number of players: *2–4* • Time to play: *90 minutes* • Complexity: *Medium*

Rehired as an architect, Butts continued working on the game in his spare time. He added a board and conducted an exhaustive study of words from the *New York Times* and other publications to figure out which letters should appear more frequently than others.

Inspired by the craze for crosswords, he renamed his game Criss Cross Words and relaunched it. Sales were just as bad.

After World War II ended, Butts sold the rights for the game to retired federal government worker James Brunot, who had played Criss Cross Words before the war and wanted to turn the game into a business. Brunot tweaked the board and rules, changed the name to Scrabble, and, like Butts, he and his wife assembled the sets at home. He sold just 2,413 copies in 1949 and 4,859 in 1951 and was ready to throw in the towel.

A lucky fluke changed everything. An order for 2,500 copies arrived from Macy's department store in New York, followed by a larger order the following week. Apparently, Jack Straus, chairman of the store, had played the game on vacation. Where Macy's led, others followed, and demand rocketed. Unable to keep up, the Brunots licensed the production and marketing rights to Selchow & Righter, the number-three game company in the US, and one that had turned down the game in 1949.

Game manufacturer Milton Bradley spent World War II making universal joints for fighter planes, as well as a kit of games for soldiers. It earned the company $2 million.

The instruction booklet in the deluxe edition of Scrabble announced the game as "ALL THE BEST WORD GAMES ROLLED INTO ONE."

As Scrabble became more popular, its production quickly outgrew the space in Brunot's home.

The deluxe edition of Scrabble also included a scoring error, which was brought to light by letters written to US *Life* magazine in January 1954.

In 1953, the year it took over producing Scrabble, Selchow & Righter sold a reported two million copies. A triumph for plastic mass production? Not at all. Standard Scrabble sets in the US have always had wooden tiles, and still do. But James Brunot had kept the rights to produce a deluxe edition of the game, which arrived on the shelves of Macy's in late 1953 in a red, leatherette box. Inside were special scoring racks made of black plastic and a set of white, chunky, plastic tiles. This would cost you $9.98, or more than three times the price of a regular Scrabble set. Compared to wood in the early 1950s, plastic was still a luxury item.

Above: MB Games Mouse Trap box from 1994.

Mechanized Mouse Trap

European companies were still recovering from the effects of the war, hobbled by shortages of materials, so it was American companies that made the most of the new wonder material. The game that defined the era, in terms of showing what game could be created when a designer's imagination was let loose, was Mouse Trap.

Mouse Trap is what is known as a Rube Goldberg machine: a massively overcomplicated device designed to perform a very simple task, named after the cartoonist who drew many such fictitious inventions.

Left: Game of Mouse Trap in play. Turning the crank triggers a chain reaction that should trap the green mouse inside the cage.

MOUSE TRAP • Year/period created: *1963* • Designer: *Marvin Glass* • Place of origin: *US* • Number of players: *2–4* • Time to play: *60–90 minutes* • Complexity: *Low*

TWISTER • Year/period created: *1966* • Designer: *Reyn Guyer Jr.* • Place of origin: *US* • Number of players: *2–4* • Time to play: *10 minutes* • Complexity: *Low*

Legendary product designer Marvin Glass, whose company created Mouse Trap, gave Goldberg credit for inspiring the game, but nothing else, and then based two more designs on his ideas (Crazy Clock Game in 1964 and Fish Bait in 1965). Goldberg, who by this time was old and ill, resisted taking Glass to court over what could be deemed to be blatant plagiarism.

Mouse Trap is a triumph of style over substance. It's a towering construction of 24 parts that refuses to be constrained by the game board below it. It looks amazing, the craziness of the giant machinery and the will-it-won't-it progress of the ball is always a delight, but nobody played the game very much because the original edition, with rules by Hank Kramer of the Ideal Toy Company, was a simple roll-and-move game with no possible strategy. In 1975, Ideal brought in the great game designer Sid Sackson to improve it: he added pieces of cheese cards that allowed players to move each other onto the "cheese wheel" space of doom. But even Sackson couldn't make Mouse Trap a decent game. There was only one place where it blew the competition away: on television.

It's hard to make a board game look exciting in a TV advertisement. Most are flat and take much longer than the length of a commercial to explain. But Mouse Trap's bizarre design and chaotic action naturally suited the small screen. Ideal Toys launched the game in the Pittsburgh area in 1963, running TV ads in the area. Three million copies sold in the first year.

Tangled up in Twister

Another game that owed a lot of its success to TV is the players-as-pieces classic Twister. The original idea came from Reyn Guyer Jr., who worked with experienced toy designer Charles Foley to create a game they called Pretzel. Along with seven other ideas, they pitched it to various companies including Milton Bradley Games. MB Vice President Mel Taft liked the game but hated the name, changing it to Twister. Production was started, television ads were booked, a marketing company hired, and the game was demonstrated at trade shows nationwide.

It didn't go well. Potential retailers were worried about the game's potentially controversial and risqué reputation—stoked by MB's rivals—

Reyn Guyer Jr. never created another hit game, but he did invent the Nerf ball in 1969.

Twister's giant "boards" were printed by a company that usually made vinyl shower curtains.

The game that ties you up in knots!

Twister

Kids | AGE **6+** | 10 | 2+ PLAYERS | ADULT ASSEMBLY REQUIRED.

Above: Colorful box art for Twister, more recently marketed very clearly as a children's game.

and when retail giant Sears Roebuck declined to include the game in its Christmas range, it looked like the end for Twister. The TV ads were canceled, and copies were pulled from stores. But the marketing company had already been paid and had landed the game a spot on *The Tonight Show* with Johnny Carson. On the evening of May 3, 1966, Carson played Twister on the show with glamorously dressed actress Eva Gabor. The next day, all remaining copies of the game sold out in New York, and by December, MB was manufacturing 40,000 sets a day to keep up with demand.

A one-off, Twister became one of the defining games of the 1960s, and no other game has been able to replicate its success at turning its players into the main components of the game. Others have tried, and Yogi (by British designer Bez, published by Gigamic in 2017) puts a clever modern twist on it, with cards instead of a mat and spinner. 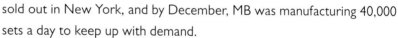 Nevertheless, Twister remains unique.

Acquiring Acquire and TwixT

One of the companies that Guyer Jr. and Foley had unsuccessfully pitched to was the Minnesota Mining and Manufacturing Company, a name that was usually shortened to 3M. Known for inventing masking tape, sticky tape, reflective signs, and Post-it notes, amongst other innovations, it may seem like an odd choice. However, in 1962, it had taken the step of setting up a division to publish board games—not an obvious move, but 3M was well known for being ahead of the curve.

ACQUIRE • Year/period created: **1964** • Designer: **Sid Sackson** • Place of origin: **US**
Number of players: **3–6** • Time to play: **60–90 minutes** • Complexity: **Medium**

Despite the booming market for children's games, 3M chose to aim its range at grown-ups. The 3M Bookshelf Games series was packaged in boxes designed to look similar to high-quality large-format books, with elegant spines that displayed when the games were stored on a shelf. The games had high production value, with well-made plastic components and intelligent game play. The more mature market for the games meant that 3M could charge a higher price than for a family game.

The company commissioned two people to design the line's first releases: Alex Randolph, a former advertising copywriter and dan-level player of Japanese game Shogi, and Sid Sackson, an engineer. At the time, neither had published a game, but between them they would lay the foundations for the modern game industry. Most of their games are still in print today, and they were among the first auteur game designers. Together, they shaped the 3M line, creating mostly abstract games, reworkings of classics, and economic simulations. 3M's first release was Sackson's Acquire, a game about building chains of hotels across a gridded board of numbered squares and acquiring shares in them.

For decades, games have described themselves in a similar way, with the following even printed on the front cover of Othello:

"A minute to learn, a lifetime to master."

This describes Acquire perfectly. The mechanics are simple but the tactics less so: just as you think you've got on top of the game's layers, you realize there's a whole new level of strategy to appreciate. There are random elements, like drawing tiles, but they're carefully balanced, so luck rarely plays a significant part. It's difficult for one player to get far ahead, and it's possible for a player to come from behind for a surprise win, and nobody gets knocked out. These are all facets of game design that would become the foundation stones of Eurogames over the next two decades.

The other notable title in 3M's first releases was Alex Randolph's TwixT, a game of placing pegs in a board and connecting them with links, trying to be first to connect opposite sides of the board. It looks simple

In the original 3M edition, Acquire's board and tiles were plastic, although later, cheaper editions have replaced them with cardboard.

Acquire itself has rarely been out of print and is available in handsome editions in Europe and cardboard editions in the US.

but is devilishly tactical and has its world championship at the annual Mind Sports Olympiad. It's less loved and harder to find, but no less good.

Sid Sackson's legacy

The 3M Bookshelf Games series ran for 13 years and released 28 titles, including Oh-Wah-Ree—which introduced a version of Mancala to American audiences—as well as boxed sets of Backgammon, Chess, and Go.

Above: Sid Sackson in his office at home in the 1990s, surrounded by some of his board game collection.

At the auction of Sid Sackon's collection, experts were not contacted to sort or describe the games, and the auction catalog was little more than a title listing.

Of the 28 titles, Randolph and Sackson contributed six each, with spin-off lines for sports and paper games. By 1976, however, the market had changed, and 3M sold the division to the war-games company Avalon Hill. Sackson went on to design award-winning games and write books, including *A Gamut of Games* and *Beyond Competition*, about cooperative game designs, published 25 years before such games became popular.

Like many designers, Sackson was a game fanatic and accumulated a collection of more than 18,000 titles, cataloged meticulously and displayed floor to ceiling in almost every room of his home in the Bronx. He was reportedly burgled several times, although the thieves never took a single game! Ian Livingstone (coauthor of this book) had previously visited Sid and his wife, Bernice, at their home to see this remarkable collection. Sid's dream was to see it in a museum, but sadly that wasn't to be. By the late 1990s, Sid's health was failing, and he could no longer manage his collection. Reluctantly, his family decided it should be put up for auction. There were medical bills to pay. Sid died on November 6, 2002, nine days before the auction. When Livingstone heard about the sale, he flew to New York, buying as many games and books as he could carry back to the UK. He laments how, in a matter of hours, thousands of games, 500 books (many rare editions), and Sid's life work went under the hammer. Sadly, it was game over.

TWIXT • Year/period created: *1962* • Designer: *Alex Randolph* • Place of origin: *US* • Number of players: *2–4* • Time to play: *30 minutes* • Complexity: *High*

Play School

Game play got serious in 1959 with the release of two new war games, Risk and Diplomacy. The idea of play was also getting serious in academic circles throughout the 20th century, with the emergence of new disciplines studying why and how we play.

War games had changed since Kriegsspiel and Little Wars (see pp.78–83). Transformed with new ideas, they moved out of officer-training colleges and the attics of retired majors and Napoleonic enthusiasts and into suburban living rooms. They became easier to understand but at the same time more tactical, more like simulations. There was a split between "miniatures war gaming"—using painted figures, often made of lead, over tabletops and sandpits—and "board war gaming"—a smaller-scale affair usually played with printed counters on a map or game board. Both fields were still comparatively new: the first miniatures war-gaming convention in the US in 1956 had just 14 attendees. Released in 1959, both Risk and Diplomacy are about years-long wars between mighty powers, with pieces representing military forces battling for territories on a board, but they couldn't be more different.

Taking a risk

Risk was invented by the French film director Albert Lamorisse—the only game designer to ever win an Oscar (best original screenplay for *The Red Balloon*, 1956). The game is played out on a world map, with players

**Albert Lamorisse
(1922–1970)**

Main image: Despite the boom in plastic, this 1959 edition of Risk still made use of wooden blocks. Wood and metal remained the dominant materials for game pieces for several decades: the houses and hotels in US Monopoly sets were still made of wood as late as 1958.

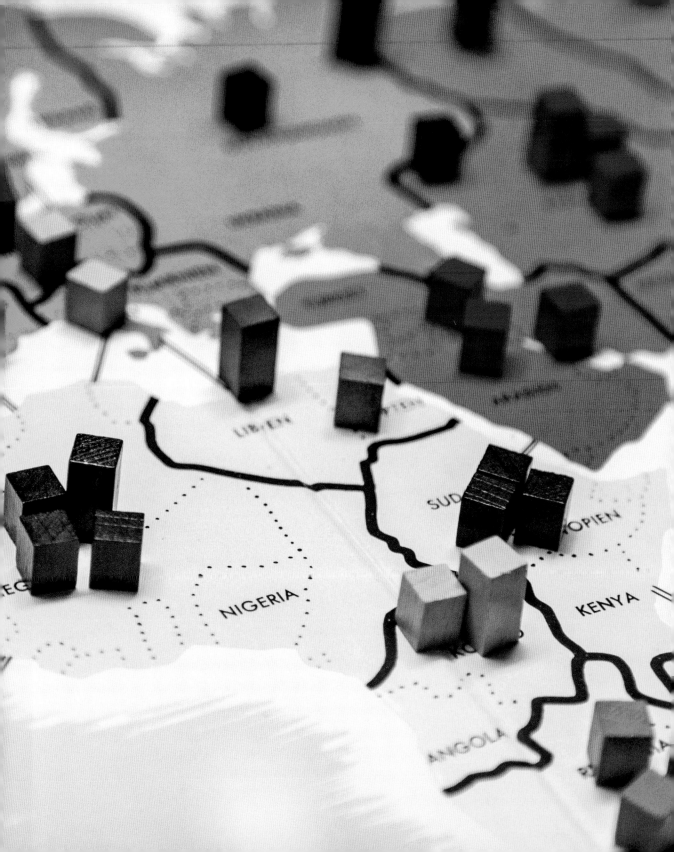

RISK • Year/period created: *1957* • Designer: *Albert Lamorisse* • Place of origin: *France* • Number of players: *2–6* • Time to play: *Approx. 2 hours* • Complexity: *Medium*

representing superpowers battling for control. It's a game of confrontation and belligerence, with lots of dice rolling and little room for subtlety. The tides of war wash back and forth across the board, sometimes for hours. There have been more than 35 different versions of the game, including Napoleonic, futuristic, umpteen versions based on movies and TV shows, and Risk Legacy, a brilliant innovation covered in chapter 18 (see p.154).

Lamorisse's first version of Risk was called *La Conquete du Monde.*

Main image: Risk, "The World Conquest Game," box and board, now with plastic troop pieces.

Diplomatic play

Diplomacy's origins are humbler than Risk's. Its creator, Allan B. Calhamer, was a postal worker who self-published the first 500 copies of his game, and over the years, it's been produced by 20 different companies, including Avalon Hill. The Diplomacy board shows "Imperial" Europe as it was in 1914 at the start of the First World War. The winner is the last player, or alliance of players, standing, but the game play is nothing like Risk's.

First, there are no dice, cards, or other random factors. The game starts evenly balanced and is all about skill and tactics, with no place for luck. Second, players don't take turns. Instead, everyone writes down their orders, then they're revealed simultaneously and resolved. If two armies clash, the larger pushes the smaller back. If they're the same size, it's a stalemate. An army is defeated and removed from the board only if it's forced into a position from where it can't retreat. Third, as its name suggests, the game has a diplomatic phase, when players find a quiet spot to negotiate alliances, treaties, and temporary pacts.

Avalon Hill was founded in 1953. Its debut game, Tactics, was the first modern war game and the first commercially successful one.

Avalon Hill's sales were in the thousands rather than the millions. Its most successful game, Gettysburg, sold 140,000 copies in its first five years— enough for the company to expand.

Left: Gibson Games UK version of Diplomacy, "The New Game of International Intrigue," box, board map of Europe, components, and rule book.

Because there are no random elements, the only way to win Diplomacy is to make deals with your opponents. Any deal is good as long as both players agree, and it stays in effect up to the moment when someone breaks it—usually by stabbing their ally in the back. Diplomacy is a game of betrayals, and has been described as being a bit like:

"stabbing your friends in the back with [a] dull, rusty knife."

LARRY HARRIS, IN *HOBBY GAMES: THE 100 BEST*

The official rule book for Diplomacy is 24 pages long.

Risk is a game classic, but Diplomacy is a masterpiece. It was the favorite game of US President John F. Kennedy, US Secretary of State Henry Kissinger and science-fiction writers Isaac Asimov and Ray Bradbury. The elegance of its mechanics influenced an entire generation of game designers, and it remains one of the purest and most intense games ever created. Diplomacy also does something very strange to the way games work, and to understand what and why that is, we have to take a jump sideways into a different field of games: academic research.

Original country unit colors:

AUSTRIA
Red

ENGLAND
Dark blue

FRANCE
Light blue

GERMANY
Black

ITALY
Green

RUSSIA
White

TURKEY
Yellow

Gaming's magic circle

In 1938, the Dutch sociologist professor Johan Huizinga of Leiden University published *Homo Ludens* ("Man the Player"), the first academic work on the study of games. Play, said Huizinga, is universal, not just to humans but to most animals, and it underlies much of human civilization. Up until this point, games had not been regarded as a serious medium

DIPLOMACY • Year/period created: *1959* • Designer: *Allan B. Calhamer* • Place of origin: *US* • Number of players: *2–7* • Time to play: *6 hours* • Complexity: *Medium*

and certainly not worthy of proper academic study. The few books about games were often concerned with just one game, usually Chess, or were general histories or collections of rules, compiled by players.

Huizinga was the first academic to examine why we play games, what play even is, and why it's so central to human life. Today, *Homo Ludens* is mostly of interest only to scholars of game studies, but two parts of it still stand out. Huizinga listed six criteria for what a game must be, and although it was written 30 years before the first video game, it still stands up remarkably well. Among the definitions, he said that play must be fun. If you play a game for any reason other than to enjoy the experience, then it isn't really a game, just an exercise that looks like a game. Think of many educational games or role-playing exercises at work. They look like games, but they exist for another reason, and so they don't feel like them.

The other key point of *Homo Ludens* is the idea of the "magic circle." Huizinga, who was big on the importance of rituals and sacred spaces, said that when we play a game, we create an invisible circle around us and inside it can do things that are not okay in everyday life. We can beat our friends. We can take their money, crush their forces, humiliate them, say horrible things to them, lie to their faces, or kill them. We can even talk about how much money we have in a way that many people find embarrassing. And we can do all of this because the game's magic circle makes it safe. When the game is over, the circle vanishes, and we return to the normal world. And we do all this without thinking about it.

This is true of 99 percent of games, but there are a few that break the magic circle. Calhamer's Diplomacy is one of them. It's famous as a game that provokes arguments, and most hobby gamers have a story about witnessing a friendship ruined by a particularly tense session. For some reason, betrayals in Diplomacy have a sharpness that can cut through the playful nature of games and continue to bleed long after the game is done. One extreme example concerns two Russian diplomats who ended up divorcing after a furious argument during a game in the 1990s. Even diplomats can fall foul of Diplomacy.

Above and left:
Illustrations from Diplomacy rule book including army and fleet movements, standoffs, convoys, and supports.

As of 2018, 11 winners of the Nobel Prize for Economics have been game theorists.

Games have gradually developed a critical vocabulary, a library of concepts and terms and ideas that describe how they work.

The magic circle is a favourite topic in game studies—the field that grew out of Huizinga's work and that of the thinkers who followed him, notably the French intellectual Roger Caillois in 1958. The parallel field of game theory—the mathematical study of competition and cooperation—had kicked off in 1928 and continued to gather momentum through the 20th century. Game studies as an academic discipline didn't get its proper kick-start until Dr. Irving Finkel's colloquium at the British Museum in 1990, but the number of books and papers on both game studies and game theory had been growing, and their ideas had been seeping back to game designers.

Building communities with Diplomacy

By the early 1960s, Diplomacy had sparked a community of people who played the game, not around a table, but by post. Everyone sent their orders to a central referee who compiled them and sent back the results. Many of these games ran turn by turn in the pages of fanzines, some set up specifically for the purpose. Editors started to review games and books and print readers' letters discussing designs and tactics. It didn't happen in an organized way, but knowledge was being shared. Instead of each designer starting from scratch to rediscover things already known in the field about game mechanics and dynamics, they could benefit directly from the established wisdom and experience of others.

In the 1970s, professional magazines like *Games & Puzzles* in the UK and *Games* in the US took the discussion further, the former providing a canvas for established designers like Sid Sackson, game historians like R. C. Bell, newcomers like future Spiel des Jahres winner David Parlett, and game fanatics like future TV personality and Member of Parliament Gyles Brandreth. Magazines informed readers about new releases, where to buy them, whether to bother, and how to find people to play them with. In the pre-internet days, they were the bulletin board of a nascent community and a billboard to nongamers that the hobby existed, albeit on a much smaller scale than today. And these magazines would help the next revolutions in game creation find an audience eager for new ways to play.

IMAGINATION

The 1960s and 1970s were a time of upheaval and change. Humans were exploring outer space, and games began to enthusiastically embrace the tropes of escapist entertainment, combined with a seemingly random influence: the effect of fantasy and science fiction.

Right: The popularity of Eurogames birthed Ticket to Ride in 2004. Starting as a train game based across the US, versions now exist set on the continents of Europe, Asia, and Africa, plus a localized New York edition, and versions with cards only and no board. **Above:** Catan and Ticket to Ride tokens.

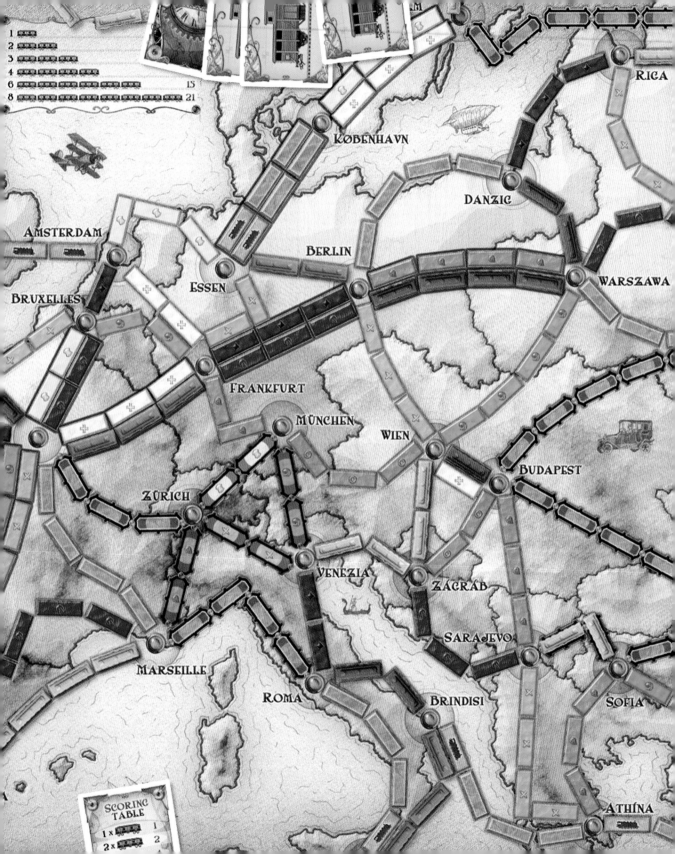

All in the Mind

In the 1960s and early 1970s, science fiction was popular, but fantasy was mostly just in paperbacks and comics. This changed with the amalgamation of fantasy novels, war games and let's-pretend games into something new.

The idea of playing a role in a game is nothing new. In his 1911 book *Floor Games*, H. G. Wells describes his sons playing as lord mayors and ship captains. The Brontë sisters created the countries of Angria and Gondal and wrote about their history, rulers, and exploits. Roles aren't even new to board games: everyone in Monopoly is a ruthless property tycoon, and in Clue you solve the murder as Professor Plum or Miss Scarlett or another of the six characters. But these roles are cosmetic: they all have the same abilities, and the role isn't the point of playing. In a tantalizing glimpse of something that sounds more modern, the game scholar Marco Arnaudo found references to Ariosto's Labyrinth, a game from 1670. In it, "each player comes to symbolise a hero, each die roll an event caused by Fortune, each event a serious or amusing allegory." It sounds like the Game of the Goose with character-based role-play.

American origins of Dungeons & Dragons

More than three centuries after Ariosto's Labyrinth came the first modern role-playing game (RPG), though it didn't use the term "role-play" on its cover—in 1974, nobody would have understood what that meant. The game was Dungeons & Dragons (D&D), and its first edition claimed to be "rules for fantastic medieval wargame campaigns, playable with pencil and paper and miniature figures." The product was a set of three digest-sized

Clue's Miss Scarlett and Professor Plum

The impact of D&D means its terms have entered everyday speech, such as leveling up, critical hits, saving throws, and magic missiles.

Main image: Original Dungeons & Dragons box art from 1974. *Additional images:* Selection of polyhedral dice used to determine the outcomes of actions in Dungeons & Dragons game play.

DUNGEONS & DRAGONS • Year/period created: *1974* • Designer: *Dave Arneson and Gary Gygax* • Place of origin: *US* • Number of players: *4–7* • Time to play: *Many hours* • Complexity: *Medium*

books, and within its pages was a whole world. D&D lets its players assume the roles of heroes in a realm of swords and sorcery, where they undertake mighty deeds in quest of glory and treasure. And although the game uses floor plans and miniature figures to keep track of the action, the majority of play is done verbally. A Dungeon Master tells players what their characters can see, and players respond or discuss their situation and make plans as though they are their characters.

Most games have a restricted set of possible actions that players can perform, but D&D lets its characters do anything they can think of: explore ruins, fight, thieve, haggle with storekeepers, lie to guards, skulk in shadows, cast hundreds of spells, and much more.

The original edition was not so much a game as a loose collection of rules; then as now, the best way to learn was from an experienced player. But that wasn't the only thing that made D&D hard to understand. It was an entirely new style of play, as different from what had come before as Monopoly is from Backgammon. It's hard to overstate how extraordinary this was. New games come out every day, but new game mechanics—the parts of the underlying systems that make games work—are much more infrequent.

D&D's cocreators, Dave Arneson and Gary Gygax, were long-time war gamers. Back in 1971, Gygax had written the Chainmail rules for medieval warfare with his neighbor Jeff Perrin. Chainmail was published by a company in their hometown of Lake Geneva, Wisconsin, and was the first commercial game to have rules for Tolkien-inspired fantasy war games. D&D was influenced by Chainmail, but its element of role-playing came mainly from Dave Arneson. Arneson had started gaming in Wisconsin in the late 1960s, where a referee named Dave Wesely had devised a narrative form of war game he called Braunstein. Wesely had taken the idea of midgame negotiating from Diplomacy (see p.114) and the concept of a referee from the text of an 1880 war game to make Braunstein base more around characters and story lines than any war game had been up to that point. Arneson developed Braunstein further, bringing in ideas from fantasy novels and rules from Chainmail.

A single game or "adventure" of D&D is normally played over several sessions. A series of adventures is called a campaign.

There have been two movies based on Dungeons & Dragons and the game's core books have hit the *New York Times* bestseller list.

Each player creates their own D&D character with statistics for six basic abilities: strength, dexterity, constitution, intelligence, wisdom, and charisma.

Above: A typical D&D set has 7 dice, each for particular scenarios. There is a D20 (with 20 sides), a D12, two D10s, a D8, a D6, and a D4.

Gygax and Arneson had known each other since 1969 and had even developed a set of naval war-game rules together, but it wasn't until 1972 that Arneson showed his friend the game he now called Blackmoor. Fascinated, Gygax asked for a copy of the rules, only to get the response, "Rules? What rules!??!" Gygax took charge of the project, organized its structure, and put together a manuscript for the game in a few weeks, testing and revising it with friends in a mighty dungeon of his own design, which he called Greyhawk. When Arneson's friend Don Lowry (who had published Chainmail) sent him samples of a new product—polyhedral dice with 4, 8, 12, and 20 sides—Arneson quickly saw their potential and built them into the game.

"Rules? What rules!??!"
DAVE ARNESON

D&D rule books "Monsters and Treasure", "The Underworld and Wilderness Adventures," and "Men and Magic"

The two designers offered the game to Avalon Hill, which turned it down. If the game industry has one recurring motif, it's established companies not realizing that they're looking at the Next Big Thing. So Gygax set up a company with friends from his war-games group, and they released the game themselves. Their new company, Tactical Studies Rules (TSR), printed 1,000 copies of the game, and it took a year to sell them all.

Dungeons & Dragons was never a smash hit. In fact, the idea behind the game spread faster than the game itself, and in the same way that people had made their own versions of The Landlord's Game, groups concocted their own rules to play this new type of game that they'd heard about. But sales of Dungeons & Dragons did increase steadily, as did the game's reputation.

Accusations of links to Satanism in the 1980s may have hurt the game's distribution, but they only increased its profile, and TSR grew to be the center of an entirely new branch of the game industry. If you bought a copy of that first printing of D&D and have kept it in good condition, it's worth more than $20,000 today.

Dungeons & Dragons in Europe

In 1975, on the other side of the Atlantic, three partners in a fledgling UK game company called Games Workshop were operating out of a small apartment in Shepherds Bush in London. They were selling their own handmade versions of Go, Backgammon, and Mancala and publishing a fanzine called *Owl & Weasel*. They heard about this new D&D game and got hold of a copy. Ian Livingstone (coauthor of this book) and Steve Jackson quickly became obsessed by it; John Peake less so. Gary Gygax of TSR had seen a copy of *Owl & Weasel* and wrote to Games Workshop. Correspondence began between the two start-ups, but it was hardly what you would call big business. An initial order for six copies of D&D resulted in TSR giving Games Workshop a three-year exclusive distribution agreement for the game for Europe. This was a pivotal moment for Games Workshop and its three partners. Led by the two D&D fanatics, the company began to specialize in science-fiction and fantasy games. John Peake, unhappy with the change in direction, left the company early in 1976.

Livingstone and Jackson's hunch paid off, and the company grew, largely on the back of D&D and other American RPGs that they were distributing. In 1977, they started a magazine, *White Dwarf*, to support the burgeoning community of RPG players in the UK. The next year, their first retail shop opened in west London, and in 1979, they founded Citadel Miniatures with Bryan Ansell in Newark, near Nottingham, to provide a range of metal figures to accompany the games. Games Workshop produced UK editions of the best American RPGs, including D&D, RuneQuest, Call of Cthulhu, and Traveller. In 1979, Livingstone and Jackson turned down a merger proposition with TSR, opting for Games Workshop to remain independent. This refusal lost them the exclusive European distribution rights for D&D.

The outcome of actions in the game is generally determined by rolling dice, but factors like a character's ability are also taken into account.

Above: Ian Livingstone, John Peake, and Steve Jackson, founders of Games Workshop, pictured in 1975.

In 1985, Games Workshop's head office moved to the heart of England, opening the renowned Warhammer World visitor center in 1997.

Left: Customers waiting for the opening of the first Games Workshop store, London, April 1978.

Warmhammer

Above: The first-ever Warhammer cover. The designers behind Warhammer were Bryan Ansell, Richard Halliwell, and Rick Priestley.

In Warhammer, miniature characters and vehicles are moved around a physical model battlefield with scaled trees, buildings and other landmarks.

Playable armies in Warhammer include creatures such as Dark Elves, Dwarfs, Lizardmen, Orcs and Goblins, and Vampire Counts.

By 1985, Livingstone and Jackson's series of *Fighting Fantasy* solo gamebooks, published by Penguin Books, had became an international hit. Running Games Workshop during the day and writing *Fighting Fantasy* gamebooks at night was beginning to take its toll, so they handed the day-to-day management of the company over to Bryan Ansell, who had been running Citadel Miniatures. Ansell was not a role-player, he was a miniatures war gamer who loved what he called his "toy soldiers."

With Games Workshop no longer the exclusive distributor of D&D, Ansell switched the company's focus to two products that had been created by Games Workshop: Warhammer (which had actually been released in 1983) and Warhammer 40,000. These were respectively a fantasy and a science-fiction battle system, each with dedicated ranges of Citadel miniatures. They were previewed and advertised in *White Dwarf* and sold in Games Workshop stores up and down the UK. The shops doubled as clubhouses where players could meet, learn the rules, play the games, get painting tips, and buy the latest products from expert staff. Customers couldn't get enough of the Games Workshop "experience" in the stores, which over time became outlets purely dedicated to Warhammer.

This shift in direction was a stunning success for the company. Ansell, Livingstone, and Jackson eventually left, following a management buy-out in 1991, and in 1994, managing director Tom Kirby floated the company on the stock market, valuing it at £35 million ($53.6 million). Kirby since stepped aside, but Games Workshop has grown ever since, and in 2018 it entered the FTSE 250 with a market capitalization of more than £1 billion ($1.3 billion).

Warhammer is set in a dark, grim version of Europe during the early Renaissance. Warhammer 40,000—or 40K as it's known—takes place in a Gothic version of outer space. Each is populated by races who are locked in eternal conflict. The slogan of 40K's box runs, "In the grim darkness of the far future, there is only war." The two games mirror each other:

WARHAMMER • Year/period created: *1983* • Designer: **Games Workshop** • Place of origin: *UK*

Number of players: *2 or more* • Time to play: *Many hours* • Complexity: *Medium*

Warhammer has the Empire and 40K the Imperium; there are Orcs and Orks; where Warhammer has types of elves, 40K has Eldar; and the forces of Chaos rampage through both universes. Critically, in neither game are the humans the goodies. In fact, there are no goodies. There is only war.

Warhammer's miniatures—originally an alloy called "white metal" but mostly plastic these days—are spectacular. The game's rules have evolved since their first edition. They grew more complex, then slimmed down again to become simpler and more accessible. Warhammer 40K is now on its eighth edition. Warhammer doesn't have an edition any more: in 2015, Games Workshop ended the game line in a cataclysmic battle that destroyed the world. Fans were displeased (to say the least). However, the void was replaced by Warhammer: Age of Sigmar, which revised the setting, imagery, and rules to create a wholly new game. Many disgruntled fans tried it and admitted that it's really very good.

Games Workshop also brought its designs to mainstream board games. In 1989, it collaborated with MB Games on HeroQuest, in which four adventurers explore a dungeon in search of treasure and glory, in a style familiar to D&D players and with recognizable elements from the Warhammer world as well. It was followed by Space Crusade, a science-fiction game using species from 40K, and by Advanced HeroQuest, which had more detailed rules than the original HeroQuest. All the games were successful and, because they were never reissued, are highly collectible today.

HeroQuest and Space Crusade were released across Europe, as well as in Australia and New Zealand. Some foreign editions made changes. In Germany, for example, Space Crusade became StarQuest, while the aliens became chaos robots. These were not killed or destroyed, but removed from this dimension or slowed down to nothing by a zero-time gun, which in other editions is clearly an assault cannon. The German version was a kinder, gentler, distant future of war. But then German game culture and tastes were growing in a different direction to the rest of Europe, in new and interesting ways.

Lady Olynder miniature

In 2011, thousands of people were introduced to Games Workshop, courtesy of a new range of Citadel miniatures based on *The Lord of the Rings*™ film trilogy.

The Space Marine character

The opening of a new Warhammer store in Hong Kong in 2018 saw Games Workshop reach the milestone of 500 stores worldwide.

Below: First edition of Warhammer: Age of Sigmar game with book, four laminated pages of rules, two range rules, a ruler, dice, and miniatures that players assemble and paint themselves.

International Spieltage

While the English-speaking game world had been obsessing over plastics and dragons, and in some cases both, a quiet revolution had been happening in Germany, and it gave way to a renowned competition.

U p until World War II, Germany was part of the same game culture as the rest of Europe, with a fluid exchange of ideas and designs. But in the postwar years, there was a shift. While a large part of the British and American game audience was happy to relive the war in their games, there was understandably little appetite for such titles in Germany. Over time, this evolved into downplaying any emphasis on direct conflict. This made it rarer for players to be knocked out halfway through, so everyone stayed in the game until the end, which proved to be more fun. However, nobody wants to be stuck in a game where it's obvious from early on who's going to win, so creators balanced their designs to avoid runaway winners. These elements came together to form a new style of game design, with an emphasis on strategy and cooperation rather than dice rolling and crushing enemies. In 1978, a group of game reviewers in Germany came together to create an award for what they considered the game of the year. It was not necessarily for the best game but was for the one that best showed what games could be. They gave themselves certain

Main images: The popularity of Eurogames led to Ticket to Ride in 2004—a game considered a great "gateway game"—perfect for introducing new players to a new and increasingly popular style of game play. This engrossing adventure of building railways and running trains across continents is actually a set-making game, not a million miles from the card game Rummy.

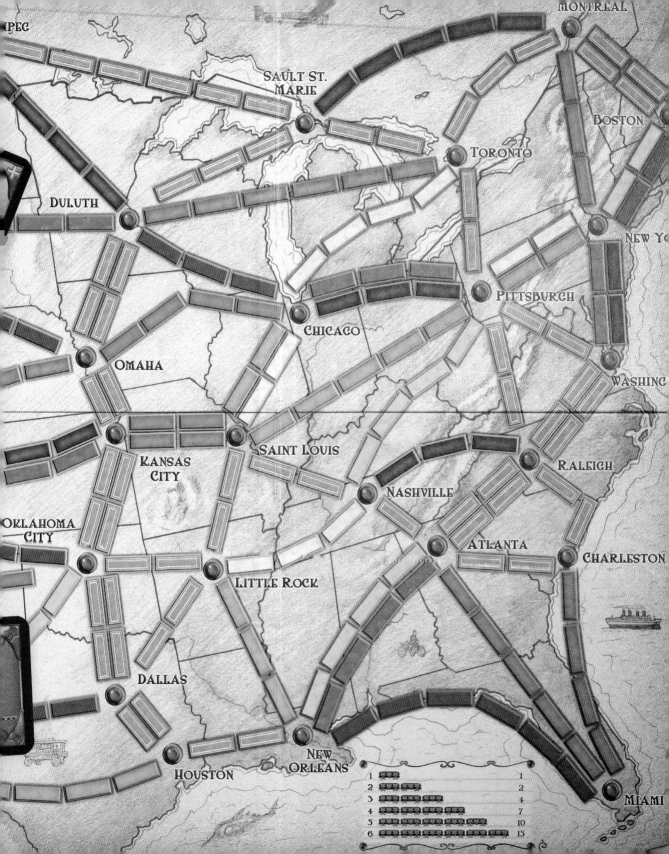

HARE AND TORTOISE • Year/period created: *1974* • Designer: *David Parlett* • Place of origin: **UK**

Number of players: **2–6** • Time to play: **Approx. 45 minutes** • Complexity: *Medium*

restrictions: the game must be analogue (not digital), available in the German language, sold in German-speaking countries and suitable for families. Winning was to bring only prestige, no cash prize. They named the award *Spiel des Jahres* (Game of the Year).

Slow and steady wins the race

The first Spiel des Jahres winner was neither German nor new. It was Hare and Tortoise, a game by British designer David Parlett, which had first been published in the UK in 1974. Four years later, Ravensburger released it in Germany as *Hase und Igel* (Hare and Hedgehog). It's a race game like Snakes and Ladders, except it couldn't be more different if it tried.

Hare and Tortoise uses neither dice nor random elements. It has a board with 65 spaces, and each player begins with 65 carrots. Moving one space takes one carrot, but moving two spaces needs three (2+1), three spaces needs six (3+2+1), and so on. Luckily many of the spaces along the board let you get more carrots in clever ways. The simplest are carrot spaces: spend a turn on one to get 10 carrots. Spaces with numbers on them are a gamble: at the start of your next turn, if the number on the space you're on matches your position in the race, then you get that many carrots times 10—so if you're on a "5" space and fifth in the race, you get 50 carrots. This favors people who aren't doing well, since they can get more carrots than the front-runners. It also means that other players can plan their move in order to ruin your chances.

Add in lettuces, hares and tortoise (or hedgehog) squares that have to be approached backward, and the result is a fascinating game. It's fast moving and simple enough for families to enjoy but with enough strategy to keep more experienced gamers happy. Every player has multiple

Hare and Tortoise board, cards and pieces

David Parlett went on to craft many more board games, including Chinese Take-Away in 2017, in which players move counter pieces with chopsticks!

options on each turn, so the race is finely balanced, and the finish is often a nail-biter. The Spiel des Jahres jury scored a hit with their first winner, though the announcement of the inaugural Spiel des Jahres was a nonevent since the organizers failed to organize a ceremony and instead postponed the whole thing for a year. Even in 1979, Parlett didn't hear about the award or learn his game had won until American board-game creator Alex Randolph told him over a meal in London some weeks later. Subsequently, Parlett says that the award has meant "pretty well everything" to him professionally. Royalties from *Hase und Igel* meant he could concentrate entirely on game design in the 1980s, and the recognition he received from the award has made him well known in the German game industry, even though none of his games have been nominated for the award since.

The rise of Eurogames

The Spiel des Jahres runs annually and has grown in stature every year. It has anointed many modern classics, from Settlers of Catan, Carcassonne, and Ticket to Ride to Dixit and Codenames. Joined by the Kinderspiel (for children's games) in 2001 and the Kennerspiel (connoisseurs' games) in 2011, the award now has international recognition, and winning can add as many as half a million extra sales to a title. It's the biggest deal in tabletop games. The Games 100 and Mensa Select badges are important, but nothing means as much for status or sales as the distinctive Spiel des Jahres red, blue, and gray *poppel* (playing pawn) with its gold wreath on the cover of a game.

Above and below:
Dixit uses picture cards to tell stories, and uses stories to work backward to identify the correct picture card.

Dixit packaging and game, illustration by Marie Cardouat

DIXIT • Year/period created: **2008** • Designer: **Jean-Louis Roubira** • Place of origin: **France** • Number of players: **3–6** • Time to play: **30 minutes** • Complexity: **Low**

133

Left: Original edition of Ticket to Ride, set in the US in the early 20th century. Players collect cards to claim train routes, connect cities, and collect points.

TICKET TO RIDE • Year/period created: **2004** • Designer: **Alan R. Moon** • Place of origin: **US**
Number of players: **2–5** • Time to play: **30–60 minutes** • Complexity: **Medium**

The Spiel des Jahres is partly responsible for bringing German games to the English-speaking market, first in the form of imports with typed, photocopied translations of the rules tucked inside the shrink-wrap, and then in proper English-language editions. The award was seen as a badge of quality for a game (though there have been a couple of stinkers over the years), and it introduced players to this new European style of gaming—giving them the unofficial title of Eurogames.

There is no hard definition for Eurogames, but the term encompasses any game, no matter where it was designed, that follows the school of game design pioneered in Germany in the last half-century. It should have easily grasped rules, depend on strategy rather than luck, lack direct confrontation, and require collaboration for progression. It should also have high-production values that often include lovely wooden pieces, such as meeple.

Meeple (the singular is the same as the plural) have become the symbol of modern games: a small two-dimensional everyperson made out of wood, with arms and legs akimbo as if star-jumping. Meeple first appeared in Carcassonne (2000) where they could represent knights, farmers, robbers, or monks. A forerunner to meeple, with a different shape but a similar idea, appeared in Heimlich & Co., known in English as

Ticket to Ride also has editions featuring Africa, Asia, Europe, France, Germany, India, the Netherlands, Nordic Countries, the UK, and New York.

Ticket to Ride ticket card and trains

Heimlich & Co. spies meeple

Carcassonne meeple

Top Secret Spies, where the pieces were shady secret agents on the trail of hidden information. The designer of this simple but brilliant game of hidden identities and sudden twists was Wolfgang Kramer. He is a pioneer of Eurogame-style design and is one-half of the great contest in modern gaming—the race to be king of the Spiel des Jahres, with more wins than anyone else.

Kramer and Teuber crowned kings

Wolfgang Kramer's first Spiel des Jahres win was Heimlich & Co. in 1986, which introduced not just meeple but another staple of modern Eurogames: the scoring track around the edge of the board. He won again the next year for *Auf Achse* (On the Axle), a game of trucking goods across Europe that hasn't aged well. And he was nominated again in 1988 for Forum Romanum, but he missed out on the hat trick when he was beaten by Barbarossa, a game of making shapes out of plasticine and sticking arrows in them, by new designer Klaus Teuber.

Barbarossa was fun, but it looked like a novelty game. Few people expected Teuber, a dental technician from Darmstadt, to amount to much. Yet Teuber confounded the critics by winning again in 1990 with *Adel Verpflichtet* (Hoity Toity)— a genteel game of collecting and occasionally stealing antiques—and then again in 1991 with *Drunter und Drüber* (Under and Over)—insane town planning with a heavy emphasis on public restrooms and shouting. Teuber had taken the crown.

Kramer, despite being mentioned by the judges both years, couldn't score another victory. He was nominated again in 1995, only to see Teuber take the award for his mighty Settlers of Catan. It was 4–2 to the dental technician, and he looked like he'd be declared the definitive designer of the decade, but Kramer stormed back in 1996 with El Grande, codesigned with Richard Ulrich. This game of controlling provinces

Above: Carcassonne's board is built as the game progresses by playing land tiles. It's a strategic game of mapmaking in Medieval France.

CARCASSONNE • Year/period created: *2000* • Designer: *Klaus-Jürgen Wrede* • Place of origin: **Germany** • Number of players: **2–5** • Time to play: **30–60 minutes** • Complexity: **Medium**

SETTLERS OF CATAN • Year/period created: *1995* • Designer: *Klaus Teuber* • Place of origin: *Germany*

Number of players: *3–4* • Time to play: *60–120 minutes* • Complexity: *High*

in Medieval Spain, with serious strategy and an enormous wooden tower, is one of the most complicated games to ever win the Spiel des Jahres, but it's also one of the best.

Then in 1999, Kramer and his collaborator Michael Kiesling produced Tikal, a masterpiece of exploring ruined temples in the jungles of central America, which won him a deserved fourth victory. The scores were leveled. Teuber was occupied expanding his empire of Catan, leaving Kramer and Kiesling an open goal in 2000, which they duly filled with Torres, an elegant game of building towers and maneuvering knights with attractive stacking plastic pieces.

That's where the total stands: Wolfgang Kramer has five wins to Klaus Teuber's four, but the game's not over. Both designers are still releasing new designs, though neither has had a win since 2000. In the 40 years of the Spiel des Jahres, between them they've accounted for more than 20 percent of the winning games. It's an astonishing track record.

The international reach of Catan

Any discussion about which Spiel des Jahres winner is the best will always come down to personal taste. However, if the conversation shifts to which is the most important, then there's no argument because it's Klaus Teuber's Settlers of Catan. It's the game that changed gaming, introduced Eurogames to the rest of the world, and sold 25 million copies in 20 years.

On paper, the game doesn't sound that exciting. Players each have a small tribe on an island made of hexagonal tiles and must collect resources to build new settlements and roads to connect them, which in turn lets them collect more resources from the hexagons they connect to. But there are five resources, so each turn has a trading phase where players can exchange different cards with each other—wool for brick, ore for lumber, and so on, to get the combinations they need to build. There are ports, a roving robber, special cards, and in the expansions, there are knights, traders, barbarians, gold, and more. But what makes the game work so well is the way all the parts of its design fit together to form a really engrossing process. Players always have interesting choices:

Settlers of Catan hexagonal tiles for different terrains

Wooden Catan settlement and city pieces

Road pieces for connecting settlements

Catan robber piece

build now or save up? Trade or hoard? What do you spend your resources on? Where do you build? The trading phase keeps everyone involved all the time, and tactics have to evolve and adapt as the board fills up with settlements, cities, and snaking roads. It's not so complex that newcomers feel overwhelmed, but it has enough strategy to keep players coming back.

Catan ruled the International Spieltage festival in Essen in 1995 and sold 400,000 copies, but it wasn't an instant hit outside Germany. An English-language edition published in America in 1996, but it was very brown and unattractive and failed to soar. It took several years of word of mouth before people outside hobby-gaming circles really started to notice something special about this game. A five-page article in *Wired* magazine in 2009 titled "Monopoly Killer" marked the moment that Settlers of Catan went mainstream in the US; it has since cropped up on TV shows and on the red carpet. At the 2017 Golden Globe Awards, when Kristen Bell and Dax Shepherd were asked what they were doing after the show, Shepherd replied that "We're going to play Settlers of Catan at roughly eight o'clock"—proving that Eurogames have truly landed in America.

Above: German packaging of Settlers of Catan *Right:* Hexagonal Catan board midplay. Settlements can be placed at the intersections of terrain hexes.

Catan resources cards (brick, ore, lumber, and wheat) and a library and a knight card.

See p.170 for a full list of Spiel des Jahres winners.

137

Collectible Pursuits

One game towers above all others—because it's a foot taller than most of them. The Jenga game took off at a time when there was also a thirst for trivia and a craze for a new type of gaming—collectible card games (CCG).

Despite the Jenga game's physical height, its sales figures did not initially soar. One reason for this was that it was the wrong moment for a stacking game. Dexterity games were out of fashion. In the early 1980s, the world was in the grip of an obsession with obscure facts, brought about by a printing advance that let companies make affordable games with several hundred cards and, in particular, a Canadian box of them called Trivial Pursuit. In an era of novelty, the Jenga game and Trivial Pursuit rapidly spawned lesser imitations. At the same time, a corner of the collectibles market previously viewed as nerdy began to go mainstream.

Jenga's rise

The Jenga game is brilliantly simple. The game consists of 54 almost-identical wooden blocks, which stack together to form a square-based tower. Players take turns to carefully extract one block from anywhere in the stack, then place it on the top. The game ends when the tower collapses in clattering, cathartic chaos. It's not the cleverest stacking game (Klaus Zoch's sublime Bausack, for example, is a sack of 70 wood shapes, with no two the same), but the Jenga game's test of dexterity and strategy has an enduring fascination that has made it a global success.

Despite the simplicity of the format, the origins of the Jenga game

Jenga blocks are traditionally made from hardwood, but some sets have been made from recycled fishing nets.

Main image: Scott Abbot and Chris Haney's Trivial Pursuit, which has spawned imitators and cheats—in the form of players who memorize all the answers in advance. Its success has led to multiple special editions and family editions, with questions for younger players.

Above: Photograph of inventor Leslie Scott, taken for the press pack for London Toy Fair in 1983, where Jenga was launched.

JENGA • Year/period created: *1982* • Designer: *Leslie Scott* • Place of origin: *UK* • Number of players: *1–8* • Time to play: *Approx. 15 minutes* • Complexity: *Low*

are a little obscure. It was first marketed in the UK by Leslie Scott, through her own company, and was shown at the London Toy Fair in 1983. It didn't catch on, and after two years of disappointing sales, Scott was persuaded to sell the worldwide rights to the game to a friend's brother on the understanding that his company, Pokonobe Associates, would license the game to the major Canadian toy company Irwin Toy. Scott entrusted Pokonobe to represent her and her game's best interests and Irwin Toy launched the Jenga game in Canada at the 1986 Canadian Toy Fair with great success. Today, the Jenga game is distributed in more than 90 countries by Hasbro, who acquired the US rights in 1987. More than 80 million games have been sold and Jenga has become a worldwide phenomenon.

Several people claim that the Jenga game is actually a traditional Ghanaian game that Scott and her family appropriated while living there in the early 1970s. That, Scott says, is not true: she and her family created a version of the game while living in Accra, Ghana, using blocks from a local sawmill, and called it Takoradi Bricks. They made a number of sets in the mid-1970s that they gave to friends in the ex-pat community and later back in the UK. Other people came across these sets, assumed the game was traditional, and proceeded to make copies of their own. One of these actually came to market before the Jenga game. In 1982, Games Workshop, experimenting with publishing family games, released Towerblox, a very similar but not identical game. Like the original Jenga game, it didn't sell well and is now one of the rarest of all Games Workshop products. The Jenga game is one of the most copied modern games in the world.

It's difficult to stop people from making wooden blocks, so there are countless own-brand, off-brand, and no-brand versions, usually made from cheaper wood and not quite as satisfying to play. What the makers don't say—and most copyists don't notice— is that real Jenga blocks aren't all the same size. Some are almost imperceptibly smaller than others, meaning they'll slide out of the stack more easily.

Games Workshop's Towerblox

The Jenga Giant game can stack more than 5 feet (1.5 meters) high, and the Jenga XXL cardboard game can reach more than 8 feet (2.5 meters) tall.

Left: Stack of original Jenga bricks from 1983.

Pursuing trivia

By contrast with Jenga, Trivial Pursuit's origins are prosaic. In December 1979, two journalists, Chris Haney and Scott Abbott, wanted to play Scrabble but found their set was missing some tiles, so they invented a trivia game instead. They self-published it in 1981, but like many fledgling game companies, they lost money until they sold the rights to veteran publishers Selchow & Righter, who relaunched it in 1983 and turned it into a global success. Trivial Pursuit was omnipresent in the mid-1980s, and it was difficult to escape a dinner party or gathering without someone suggesting a round of it. It sold a staggering 30 million copies by 1985 but glutted its own market. By the end of the decade, demand had reduced.

The game is simple: roll a die, move your piece, and answer a question from one of six subjects determined by the space you land on. A correct answer earns another move or, if it's a special space, a "piece of pie." The first to collect all six pieces of pie and return to the center for a final question wins. The game play is the least interesting aspect; the game would be nothing without the trivia, and if you're no good at trivia—or you're trapped on a theme you don't know—then it can be torture.

Just like Jenga, Trivial Pursuit spawned a host of imitators, clones, and knockoffs, some with a decidedly questionable grasp of facts. They weren't alone: some of the answers in Trivial Pursuit itself were wrong, as the makers discovered when they were sued by the author of several books of trivia, Fred Worth. He had included dummy facts in his books to trap copiers, and these had duly appeared on cards in the game. Worth demanded $300 million in damages, but didn't win anything in court.

Other game creators were quick to spot the possibilities of games with hundreds of cards. Balderdash, Pictionary, Taboo, Articulate!, Scattergories, I Think You Think I Think, and more all followed within a decade. Many of them were simply traditional party games in a box with a board. A Question of Scruples made a big splash in 1984 by posing moral conundrums to the players, but had almost disappeared within a few years. The format is far from dead: Apples to Apples came out from tiny publisher Out of The Box in Minnesota in 1999 and was bought

Trivial Pursuit box and board

Special editions of Trivial Pursuit include *Star Wars, Lord of the Rings,* Disney, the Rolling Stones, and the Beatles as well as family and junior editions.

Trivial Pursuit's six original categories are Geography (blue), Entertainment (pink), History (yellow), Arts & Literature (brown), Science & Nature (green), and Sport & Leisure (orange).

TRIVIAL PURSUIT • Year/period created: *1981* • Designer: *Chris Haney and Scott Abbott* • Place of origin: **US** • Number of players: **2–24** • Time to play: **90 minutes** • Complexity: **Low**

MAGIC: THE GATHERING • Year/period created: *1993* • Designer: *Richard Garfield* • Place of origin: *US*

Number of players: **2+** • Time to play: **Approx. 20 minutes** • Complexity: *High*

by Mattel for $4.5 million (£3.5 million) eight years later. Cards Against Humanity, which employs Apples to Apples rules with uncouth cards, was crowdfunded on Kickstarter in early 2011 before becoming a global smash. Wits & Wagers is a trivia game with hard questions that challenges players to guess closest to the right answer and then bet on who's guess is most accurate. And in 2015, Codenames, a clever word game of finding spies with 200 cards in its box, won the Spiel des Jahres (see p.132).

A new gathering

All of this pales into insignificance beside the card game released by a tiny Seattle company in the summer of 1993. Wizards of the Coast had been formed to publish books about role-playing games (RPGs) but soon found that market in decline. Founder Peter Adkison was approached by Richard Garfield, a mathematician and occasional game designer, who showed him a prototype board game of programming robots with hilarious consequences. The game was RoboRally. Adkison liked the design but thought it was too ambitious for his fledgling company. He asked Garfield whether he had anything that would be cheaper to produce. If it was successful, he reasoned, it might then pay for RoboRally to be published. Garfield came back with Cosmic Encounter, a card game inspired by a classic game of the late 1970s with the same name.

Cosmic Encounter is a game of conflict between multiple alien races, each trying to establish five colonies in other players' star systems. The concept is simple, but each alien race has a unique power that allows them to bend the rules in a specific way, for example, changing the turn order, reversing the results of battles, or forcibly allying with another player. Since players can choose from many different aliens, the game has endless tactical variety, so it never gets old. This is known as "exceptions-based game play," and Garfield used the idea to excellent effect in his design for a game of dueling wizards. The basic rules are easy to pick up, but each card works in a slightly different way, for example, causing damage, summoning monsters, allowing players to bring back discarded cards, and hundreds of other possibilities. This game was called Magic:

Cosmic Encounter planet and ship pieces

Magic: The Gathering Deckmaster box

The success of Magic: The Gathering and its imitators pushed collectible card games into the mainstream.

Magic: The Gathering is often considered as complex as Calhamer's strategy game Diplomacy.

The Gathering, and the genius way it was sold caused it to become the world's first collectible card game (CCG). The game was sold in decks of 60 cards or booster packs of 15, in which you received a random selection of the 295 cards that made up the complete set.

Magic turned out to be expensive to produce. Each card had a unique painting—a huge up-front cost. Wizards borrowed heavily to finance the production and offered some of its artists stock in the company in exchange for their services. It was a huge risk, but when the game launched in August 1993 at the Gen Con game convention, it was the hit of the show. People crowded five-deep around the Wizards booth to buy cards.

By the end of August, Wizards had sold its entire first print run of 2.6 million cards, which they'd thought would last them the rest of the year. They printed more … and more … and more. By the end of 1994, they had released five expansions for the game and sold a billion cards, with no sign of demand slowing down. That year, they also published RoboRally.

As with Trivial Pursuit, the market was swiftly flooded with imitators, intent on cashing in on the gold rush for card collecting games, but with patchy success. TSR's Spellfire (using old art from Dungeons & Dragons) was a notable flop. Better games followed, and for a while, the market was glutted with releases. The Pokémon Trading Card Game came out in 1999, also published by Wizards of the Coast, and demand was so high that so many card printers in the US were producing the game that there was a shortage of collectible baseball cards that year. Yu-Gi-Oh! came out in Japan in 1999 and the US in 2002 and remains a strong seller today. In 1995, TSR produced Dragon Dice, with packs of custom-made collectible dice, and 2000 saw the release of Mage Knight, a game based on the CCG model but with collectible prepainted miniature figures in place of cards.

As for Wizards of the Coast, in 1997, it bought TSR and with it Dungeons & Dragons. They launched a third edition of the role-playing game in 2000 to great acclaim and success. A year earlier, Wizards itself had been bought by the all-consuming Hasbro in a deal worth $325 million. Several artists who had accepted stock instead of cash for their Magic art were suddenly able to buy houses on the back of the deal.

THE FUTURE

For a while, it looked as if digital games would spell an end for physical board games, but the two have forged a synergy and produced hybrids that couldn't have existed before. No matter what happens in the future, as long as there are humans, there will be games, and we're sure the best are still to come.

Right: Crowdfunded games such as Exploding Kittens put the game-making process into the hands of its fans and combined the online/digital with the physical in a new way. **Above:** Elements from Codenames and Beasts of Balance.

Thinking Outside the Box

With the dawn of a new millennium came a sense of expanding horizons. While some designers were trying to put a twist on traditional games, others were thinking of alternative ways players could interact with games.

As usual, inspiration for these new games came from the past. The very earliest games in history are abstract, simply pieces on a board, but even by the time of Senet, the game play had transformed into representing the journey of souls through the afterlife. Chess pieces are modeled after specific units and officers in the Indian Army, Hnefatafl is the struggle of a king and his guard to escape from an invading force. Similarly, while the tokens in the Royal Game of the Goose don't represent much, by the 18th century, the games modeled on it implied that the players' pieces were travelers on a path—whether exploring Europe or the New World, or living the life of a respectable person from birth to death, or pilgrims on a metaphorical ride beset with temptation.

As games became more sophisticated, participants had an increasing sense that the play should be about something. Publishers also discovered it was easier to sell a game with a strong theme, an implied story, and a meaningful victory. Suffragetto (see p.92) consists of pieces on a grid, but the moment you picture the blue pieces as police and the green

Sherlock Holmes Consulting Detective artwork

Main image: Fairy-tale artwork from the box cover of storytelling game Once Upon a Time.
Additional images: Black-and-white scenes and characters from Sherlock Holmes Consulting Detective: Thames Murders & Other Cases (2017), including Holmes examining a clue, Watson writing notes, and a smoggy London scene with steamboat on the river Thames.

SHERLOCK HOLMES CONSULTING DETECTIVE • Year/period created: *1981* • Designers: *Gary Grady, Suzanne Goldberg, Raymond Edwards* Place of origin: *US* • Number of players: *2–4* • Time to play: *60–120 minutes* • Complexity: *Medium*

as suffragettes, it acquires a whole deeper meaning, and the victory feels more significant. Clue consciously follows the setup of the English country house murder mystery—made popular by Agatha Christie—with everyone a suspect. The trouble is that these games are heavy on theme and set-up, and then the game play doesn't really create a story—at least not a memorable one.

Choose your own game adventure

The first games that specifically set out to tell stories were the role-playing games (RPGs) from the 1970s. They were open-ended and not completed in a single session—even if you cleared all the monsters and treasure out of a dungeon, your character would spend their gold on better equipment and come back next time to face a tougher threat. The stories might not be great when written down, but they don't have to be; the fun is in experiencing them as they happen as impromptu theater, and in shaping the direction of the tale.

There are ongoing RPG campaigns that have been running for more than 40 years with the same players and characters in a single continuing saga.

Inspired by RPGs, there had also been a rash of storytelling games in the early 1980s. In Sherlock Holmes Consulting Detective, the players are Holmes' assistants—the Baker Street Irregulars—working together to solve a series of crimes, using newspapers and maps to help them. In fact, most of the game revolves around the "case book," a booklet with numbered paragraphs that you turn to and read out loud. It's undeniably fun and was groundbreaking on its release in 1981, but it's not much more than a multiplayer version of a solo gamebook, where each paragraph gives you a series of options at the end, and you turn to the next paragraph to see what happened.

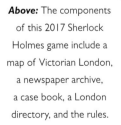

There were two hit series of solo narrative books in the early 1980s: *Choose Your Own Adventure* (CYOA) originating in the US, and *Fighting Fantasy* in the UK. The latter was created by coauthor Ian Livingstone and Steve Jackson, last seen setting up Games Workshop. Unlike the CYOA books, theirs contained an actual game system with rules for creating a character and fighting monsters. It needed dice and

Above: The components of this 2017 Sherlock Holmes game include a map of Victorian London, a newspaper archive, a case book, a London directory, and the rules.

A first edition of Jackson and Livingstone's fantasy adventure gamebook *The Warlock of Firetop Mountain*.

In 1985, Decipher, Inc produced a range of murder-mystery games, including The Chicago Caper, The Watersdown Affair, and The Last Train from Paris.

In the 1990s, Decipher, Inc. diversified into successful collectible card games based on *Star Wars*™ and *Star Trek*®. The company was almost destroyed by the revelation that the founder's brother-in-law— VP of finances— had embezzled more than $1.5 million of the company's money.

a pencil to play—a proper game, in other words, but for a single player.

The first in the series was *The Warlock of Firetop Mountain* in 1982, the story of your quest (all the books are written in the second person, present tense) to explore the dungeons under the eponymous mountain, solve its puzzles, deal with its hostile inhabitants, and finally defeat the evil warlock Zagor. Puffin Books printed a cautious 5,000 copies, which sold out immediately. The title went on to shift over two million, and the series as a whole has passed 20 million sales worldwide, with many titles including *Warlock*, *Deathtrap Dungeon*, *Forest of Doom*, *City of Thieves*, *House of Hell*, and *Sorcery!* being converted into video games and apps. Clearly, there was an appetite for a mix of story and game play, which computer games seemed happy to supply, but board games not as much.

A year later, Decipher, Inc. launched the first of its How to Host a Murder games: part dinner party, part murder-mystery. Each guest at the party receives a booklet describing their character, and then the evening is divided into several acts, with new information revealed during each one. Somewhere along the way, one of the players discovers they are the murderer—they often don't know at the beginning—and must act accordingly. It's less a game, more an exercise in guided improvised drama, but it's undeniably fun and the process of unravelling the trail of clues is very satisfying, at least in those that are well written.

The most notable board game with story elements in the 1980s was Tales of the Arabian Nights by Eric Goldberg. It involves a riotous trip around the world of Middle Eastern folklore, low on tactics but high on laughter, in which one can become hugely rich, married with children, discover legendary places of power, be imprisoned, turned into an ape, or all of the above, sometimes at the same time. It, too, is driven by a thick book full of numbered paragraphs, with a complicated system that determines what you encounter on your turn and the result of your interaction with it.

The first major game where storytelling was an integral part of the gameplay was Once Upon a Time—"the storytelling card game"— designed by Andrew Rilstone, Richard Lambert, and James Wallis

FIGHTING FANTASY • Year/period created: *1982* • Designers: *Ian Livingstone and Steve Jackson* • Place of origin: **UK** • Number of players: *1* • Time to play: **Varies** • Complexity: *Medium*

(coauthor of this book). It's a card game of telling a story using cards with fairy-tale tropes. You win by playing your ending card—each player has a different one—so you must steer the story around so yours fits what's gone before, but you can't play it until you've played all your other cards. Along the way, other players will be using their cards to interrupt you and take control of the story. Like Tales of the Arabian Nights—which was one of its inspirations—it doesn't create great stories but is very entertaining to play and has been translated into 12 languages.

Above: Examples of the cards used in the storytelling game Once Upon a Time.

Flights of fantasy

Magic: The Gathering also has a story. Each expansion includes new characters, settings, and plot elements, but the story itself doesn't come through as you're playing it. For that you need to read the official background, or the comics or novels set in the world of the game. But since its first release, every card has a text box that contains information on how it works in the game, and usually some "color text"—its lore, background, goals, or even a quotation. Players understand how that card fits into the structure of the game's mythic background.

When the hit game of the decade has narrative content on its cards, the rest of the game industry takes notice. The first reaction was to produce collectible card games (CCGs) with stories by basing them on movies, TV shows, or books with strong stories—Star Wars™, Star Trek®, The X-Files, The Lord of the Rings, and RPGs like Call of Cthulhu or the World of Darkness series that had begun with Vampire: the Masquerade in 1991. But the idea that board games could tell a developing story as you played them grew throughout the decade. The US game publisher Fantasy Flight Games championed this from its first release, 1997's six-hour epic of building empires in space, Twilight Imperium. Where a game like Cosmic Encounter gave you a pack of alien races but told you almost nothing about their culture or history,

Magic: The Gathering, released in 1993, is considered to be one of the first trading card games.

Deck-building began as a way of players choosing which cards to include in a CCG deck and came into its own in 2008 with Donald X. Vaccarino's 500-card Dominion.

150

Steve Jackson's
The Citadel of Chaos
and Ian Livingstone's
The Forest of Doom,
City of Thieves, and
Deathtrap Dungeon

Twilight Imperium contains just a handful of aliens, but each one has a rich background, with unique ships and technology, and these in turn give them advantages and disadvantages and a sense of realism. They become more than just pieces on a board; they have a heritage, a cause, and strong reasons to dislike each other.

Fantasy Flight Games went on to develop many games with rich backgrounds and stories, from the Runebound series, set in the fantasy world of Terrinoth—which is also where their Descent and Battlelore games take place—to its series of Living Card Games (LCGs), which play like CCGs but with all the cards available in each set so you don't have to spend a fortune to acquire the rare ones. Android Netrunner, one of the most successful LCGs, is a two-player game with one player as a monolithic corporation and the other a hacker trying to infiltrate its systems. Android Netrunner included expansions that were specifically marketed as "narrative," which expanded and advanced the story of the game, adding new characters and corporations.

Fantasy Flight Games also released several games based on H. P. Lovecraft's Cthulhu mythos, and specifically the version of it from the groundbreaking 1981 RPG Call of Cthulhu. This meant they weren't just story-driven; they were based on Lovecraft's specific style of strange, creeping horror, and the characters that you play in them tend to follow the same paths as Lovecraft's heroes—which usually mean going mad or meeting a terrible doom. Arkham Horror, Elder Sign, and Mansions of Madness all follow this pattern. They're also all cooperative games.

Co-play

Cooperative games are the second big change in games in the last few years. In almost all games, the player is competing against other players to be the sole winner. In a cooperative game, all the players are working together to beat the game itself: either everyone wins, or everyone loses.

The idea of competing against the game isn't new. It's how most computer games work and also games like Solitaire and Patience, although those are for one player. Cooperative games have their roots in the 1970s and 1980s, where games like Escape from Colditz, Dungeons & Dragons, Scotland Yard, and Fury of Dracula had several players working together against a single powerful adversary controlled by one player. For example, in Escape from Colditz, players are the escape committees of different nationalities, working together to foil the German security officer, and in Scotland Yard, players are the police trying to locate and capture an escaping criminal, Mr. X. Although these games have cooperative elements, they're usually known as "asymmetric," meaning players have a different range of powers and abilities. Sherlock Holmes Consulting Detective is also cooperative but is thin on actual game elements.

The first proper, cooperative game was the original Arkham Horror, released in 1987 by Chaosium, the company behind Call of Cthulhu. Players are investigators in the Massachusetts town of Arkham and must locate and close gates to other planes of reality, before a powerful entity uses them to break through to the players' world. Though fun, it was slow and complex, and after it had sold out, Chaosium did not reprint it until approached by Fantasy Flight Games, 18 years later.

Another early example of a cooperative game is Aliens (1989), based on the classic science-fiction horror movie. Players represent characters from the film, while the aliens appear randomly and behave according to a simple set of rules—they move directly toward the nearest player and then try to kill them. If the players don't work closely together, they won't last very long. Aliens captures the tense, claustrophobic atmosphere of the movie. Players don't play through the whole game in one sitting; it has "scenarios" based on particular action sequences from the film, and how a player performs in one can affect what happens next.

The cooperative game that changed everything was inspired by another movie. The Lord of the Rings game was released in 2000, shortly before the first of Peter Jackson's movie trilogy came out. The game was created by Reiner Knizia, not just one of the greatest, but also the most prolific designer of the last three decades: he has more than 600 published games to his name—many of them modern classics.

The Lord of the Rings is based on Tolkien's books, not the movies, so

Above: Author H. P. Lovecraft's 1934 sketch of a statuette depicting Cthulhu, which was the inspiration for several choose-your-own-adventure style fantasy role-play books and games.

The Hobbit and The Lord of the Rings author J. R. R. Tolkien

A Waddington cooperative game version of Thunderbirds from 1966 was potentially the very first of its genre.

the entire story is included in a single game. The players are the Hobbits of the Fellowship, each with a unique power, and must convey the One Ring to Mount Doom, pursued by Dark Lord Sauron. They must stick closely together or the Fellowship is broken; they must explore key locations from the book; and when they reach Mount Doom, the one who is carrying the ring must sacrifice themselves to let the others win the game. It turns out that cooperative games are really good at capturing the style and mood of a story, because all the players are following the same main story line instead of working against each other. The game was a huge success, and other designers jumped on the bandwagon of cooperative games, but the field had to wait a few years for its Mozart to arrive.

Matt Leacock was a user experience designer for companies such as AOL and Yahoo when his first game was released in 2008: Pandemic. Four virulent diseases have broken out around the globe, and the player is part of a team tasked with containing them, discovering a cure, and saving the world. But the contagions will spread unpredictably across the map and may have explosive outbreaks. Working as a team is essential. Pandemic demands careful strategy, planning, and coordination. It's possible to lose in just three turns (with three players having one turn each). Even when a player wins, it's likely to come down to the turn of a card, and their pulse will be racing as they slowly flip it to reveal their fate. Leacock is a master of keeping players on the edge of their seats.

It's a modern classic, but not a perfect one. Setup is long and fiddly, and because the players have to work together, there's a tendency for

RESEARCHER

• You may give any 1 of your City cards when you Share Knowledge. It need not match your city. A player who Shares Knowledge with you on their turn can take any 1 of your City cards.

OPERATIONS EXPERT

• As an action, build a research station in the city you are in (no City card needed).
• Once per turn as an action, move from a research station to any city by discarding any City card.

CONTINGENCY PLANNER

• As an action, take any discarded Event card and store it on this card.
• When you play the stored Event card, remove it from the game. Limit: 1 Event card on this card at a time, which is not part of your hand.

PANDEMIC • Year/period created: **2008** • Designer: **Matt Leacock** • Place of origin: **US** • Number of players: **2–4** • Time to play: **45 minutes** • Complexity: **Medium**

Pandemic board in play and additional role cards

RISK LEGACY • Year/period created: **2011** • Designer: **Rob Daviau** • Place of origin: **US**

Number of players: **2–4** • Time to play: **60 minutes** • Complexity: **Medium**

people who know the game to take charge and tell the others what they should do—a phenomenon known as "quarterbacking." But it's still fun.

Pandemic was as influential as The Lord of the Rings had been and has spawned several sequels. Leacock followed it up with Forbidden Island (2010), another cooperative game, with players recovering four treasures from the titular island as it slowly sinks. That is just as nail biting, and also has sequels: Forbidden Desert (2013) and Forbidden Skies (2018).

Leacock returned to the Pandemic brand in 2015 for what is probably his greatest game, Pandemic Legacy: Season 1, produced in collaboration with Rob Daviau. A former game designer at Hasbro, Daviau's credits include card game versions of classics, like Battleship and The Game of Life, and the Trivial Pursuit DVD Pop Culture board game. But in 2011, he was allowed to experiment with one of Hasbro's crown jewels, Risk, to produce something startlingly new.

Raising the Risk stakes

The idea for Legacy games came from a work meeting where Daviau jokingly asked why the characters in Clue kept getting asked back to dinner. The game, of course, has no memory: every time you play, it starts with a blank slate. What if the game's characters remembered what had happened the last time? His pitch for Clue Legacy was rejected, but he was asked to apply the idea to Risk (see also p.114).

Above: Anthony E. Pratt's Cluedo (1949) inspired the creation of a game called Clue Legacy and then, in time, Risk Legacy.

Risk Legacy is set in a postapocalyptic future. The basic game play is similar to classic Risk, but when you finish a game, the result will affect how the next session of the game begins. You may be instructed to write on the board or apply stickers. Sometimes you'll have to add new cards to the game, or even tear some up. And there are sealed compartments within the game's box that you must not open until the game tells you to, because there are surprises and secrets within.

You play Risk Legacy for 15 sessions, with the same group of players. Every session is different: powers change, rules change, the shape of the

Risk Legacy shot to the top of BoardGameGeek. com's highest-rated games and stayed there for almost two years.

Leacock and Daviau collaborated again to produce Pandemic Legacy Season 2; released in 2017.

Detail from Risk box artwork

The brains behind Gloomhaven, Isaac Childres, acquired financial support to launch his game via Kickstarter.

map changes. By the end, the board has become scarred with the history of previous conflicts, and you will have experienced one of the great journeys of modern gaming, an epic you will remember for a long time. It is a truly extraordinary game—but it's not as good as Pandemic Legacy.

Pandemic Legacy takes everything that's great about Risk Legacy and builds in all the strengths and intensity of a cooperative game; or perhaps it takes everything great about Pandemic and stretches its tension over a game year that you have to play through month by month. It's a campaign; it's an unfolding story of trying to save the world against diseases that evolve in quite horrible ways; it's a battle for raw survival.

As with Risk Legacy, there are secrets concealed inside the box, all clever, most unexpected, and some change the game utterly. It is a brilliant piece of game design and an unforgettable game to play.

Playing any Legacy game is a commitment. If players drop out after a few sessions, the experience is changed, and it's difficult to find someone to join in mid-flow. But if you do commit to playing through the whole of Pandemic Legacy: Season 1, you'll find there's no other game like it.

Those three elements—story, cooperation and Legacy-style play—are the cutting-edge game design ideas of the early 21st century. The game that knocked Pandemic Legacy off the number-one spot on BoardGameGeek.com was Gloomhaven, a massive fantasy-adventure game that almost combines all three elements to create a colossus with 95 scenarios, 17 characters to play, and more than 1,500 cards in a box that weighs almost 22 lb (10 kg). It is a time-consuming game, but then a game with a price tag of $140 should be good for more than a handful of sessions. Undoubtedly, that figure is a lot of money for a board game—far more than most people would be prepared to pay, and Gloomhaven demands levels of commitment that only serious game fans would be able to reach.

As the mainstream market caught up with hobby games in the early part of the new millennium, other hobby games streaked away again, becoming even bigger and more complicated. But the market has expanded, and there are games to fit all tastes, all levels of experience, and all budgets.

A World of Games

Exciting and innovative games weren't limited to the US and Germany. All over the world, enthusiasts were setting up companies to bring their own designs to an increasingly international market.

For much of the 1980s and 1990s, there were only a few countries where fledgling game companies catering to hobby gamers could prosper. The US and Germany had the two largest communities of hobby gamers in the world and therefore the largest markets. In other places, such as the UK, there simply weren't enough gamers to support a company that didn't sell outside its own borders, and the chances of a game breaking through to the mass market were minimal.

Moving online

Games themselves had a global appeal, and the internet stripped away borders. Newsgroups and early board-game websites shared new releases to everyone who was online, and with the start of e-commerce, ordering games from overseas became something anyone with a credit card could do.

Codenames icons

Early websites like the Games Cabinet let people download English translations of the rules for German and French games. The website BoardGameGeek.com was founded in 2000 and began compiling its massive database of board games. Today it lists descriptions, reviews, and play reports of more than 100,000 different games and has more than two million registered users. Many games are now produced in a print-and-play format, downloadable as PDFs that players print out and assemble at home.

Many countries, such as Soviet Russia, had their own thriving game industries before the internet made games global.

Main image: Artwork by Xavier Collette from Mysterium, a murder-mystery game from the Ukraine, with a genuine sense of time and place. *Additional images:* The two opposing teams from Czech Vlaada Chvátil's Codenames.

MACHI KORO • Year/period created: **2012** • Designer: **Masao Suganuma** • Place of origin: **Japan**
Number of players: **2–4** • Time to play: **30 minutes** • Complexity: **Medium**

There have always been gamers who have designed and published their own games, drawing on raw enthusiasm but not much market research. Many of the games in this book were originally self-published, only for the creator to run into financial trouble and sell the rights to someone else who turned it into a hit. Or for the game to be a hit and the creator license it to a larger publisher because they couldn't keep up with demand. Sadly, the most common story is people who produce several thousand copies of a game, only to learn that, just because their family and friends like it, it doesn't mean anyone else will. Their garages are probably still full of unsold copies to this day.

Breaking into the market, let alone the international market, may not have been easy for newcomers, but that doesn't mean that other countries hadn't been producing their own games, even if they didn't get the same attention as the German and American titles. Most countries had games produced for their local markets, and some found an international following.

In the last 10 years, Japanese games have been succeeding in the West, with titles such as Machi Koro and A Fake Artist Goes to New York. At SPIEL 2018, a company from Singapore called Capital Gains showed a range of board games based on the principles of economic theory, with titles like Wongamania, Debtzilla, and Cryptocurrency.

Above: In Machi Koro, everyone is Mayor, but only of a wheat field and a bakery. The aim of the game is to build up your town using dice and cards to complete landmarks.

Games of the Eastern Bloc

Soviet Russia had a board-game tradition dating back to its beginnings in the early 1920s. Soviet titles include Дадим сырье заводам ("We Will Give Raw Materials to the Factories," 1930), which praises children for collecting scrap fabric, iron, paper, bottles, and boots for recycling and Ленин идет в Смольный ("Lenin Goes to Smolny," 1970)—a game about protecting the Bolshevik leader from his foes during a key night of the October Revolution in 1917. These games were mostly basic fare for children but with glorious constructivist artwork on their boards. Other subjects included chemical warfare, the electrification of the country, the redistribution of materials, and many simple war games.

By 2011, politics had changed. Poland's Institute of National

An edition of newspaper *The Leningrad Metallurgist* (1930) featured cut-out-and-play elements for the children's race game We Will Give Raw Materials to the Factories.

In the 1928 game Electrification, players had to trade and place light-bulb cards in a race to be the first to electrify their section of the board (depicting villages and a port).

Remembrance published *Kolejka* (Queue), a game with a less idyllic view of the days of Communism. It was about queueing outside stores in the hopes that they'd get a delivery of something you wanted and that you'd be close enough to the front of the queue to buy some before it ran out. Cards included "Borrow a baby" (to move to the front of the queue), "This isn't your place," and "Store closed." The intent behind it, the designer Karol Madaj said, was "to show young people and remind the older ones what hard times these were and what mechanisms were at play." *Kolejka* was a surprise hit, and demand was so high that ironically there were shortages of it. After three years, it had sold 100,000 copies and was released in French and Romanian editions. There was a rumor that the game had been banned in Russia, but that turned out to be capitalist propaganda.

Poland had developed a thriving game scene, with several games breaking through to the international market. Portal Games had begun as an RPG publisher and distributor in the 1990s, but its founder Ignacy Trzewiczek soon discovered that he had a talent for board-game design. Portal Games has now become a well-respected midrange publisher, and Trzewiczek's Detective won the 2019 As D'Or for Best Expert Game at the Festival International des Jeux in France.

The former Eastern Bloc has produced several other top-notch game companies. The Czech Republic has two: Czech Games Edition (CGE) and Czech Board Games (CBG), which is as confusing as you'd expect. The former is the more successful, largely down to its lead designer Vlaada Chvátil, a former video-game creator who broke through in 2006 with Through the Ages: A Story of Civilization. A year later, he made the Spiel des Jahres "recommended" list with CGE's first release, Galaxy Trucker, a real-time game of building a spaceship out of junk parts and then racing it.

Above and below: Codenames box and game in play, where two teams battle to identify their spies' code names from a tableau of random word cards, based on single-word clues.

Decoding Codenames

Chvátil's games range from serious strategy titles like Through the Ages to light party games such as Pictomania, Bunny, Bunny, Moose, Moose, and his 2015 hit, Codenames, which won the Spiel des Jahres, sold a million copies in its first

CODENAMES • Year/period created: *2015* • Designer: *Vlaada Chvátil* • Place of origin: **The Czech Republic** • Number of players: **4–8** • Time to play: **15–30 minutes** • Complexity: **Medium**

MYSTERIUM • Year/period created: **2015** • Designer: **Oleksandr Nevskiy and Oleg Sidorenko** • Place of origin: **Ukraine** • Number of players: **2–7** • Time to play: **45 minutes** • Complexity: **Medium**

year, and has established itself as a mainstream game. Codenames is for two teams of spies. Each team has its own spymaster and a grid of 25 cards with words on them, each one a codename for a spy. The spymasters have a map showing which spies belong to which team, which cards are innocent civilians, and which is the assassin—which brings instant death.

The spymaster gives their team a one-word clue and a number, and they have to figure out which of the cards it refers to. So the clue "Palace, four" means four of the cards in the grid that refer to "Palace" are spies on your team, and you need to identify them. "Queen" almost certainly is one of them. "England," probably. "Staff"? Palaces have staff. Or "Dragon," for a fairy-tale reference? And then you notice "Crystal" and remember the English soccer team, but Aunt Bridget has spotted "Tower," and all good palaces have towers… Which four will you take a chance on? It's a party game that makes you feel clever, with that trick that the best games have of adapting its level to the people playing it—it's as fun with kids as it is with adults, or a mix of both. It deserves its success.

Ukrainian Mysterium

Elsewhere in the former Soviet Union, the Ukraine has an expanding game industry, including the world-class publisher IGAMES. It's the company behind one of the hits of the mid-2010s: Mysterium. A brilliant blend of Clue and Dixit, the game challenges players to solve a murder over seven game days, but with a twist: the clues are dreams sent to them by a ghost—another player—in the form of cards with surreal images on them. From these enigmatic images, they must deduce the identity of the murderer, the location of the crime, and the weapon.

It sounds like someone's tried to strap the front end of a stallion onto the back end of an elephant. It shouldn't work at all, yet it does, really well. Can you tell whether this mouse on a unicycle refers to the nun, the postmaster, or the retired general? Mysterium delightfully pulls off the trick of being tense and funny at the same time. IGAMES produced the

Above: Mysterium box by Libellud with components.
Below: Art from Libellud's Mysterium cards, perfectly judged to fit the mood of the game.

Ukrainian and Russian versions of the game but licensed it elsewhere. Portal Games picked up the Polish rights and released their edition before the Ukrainian one. Italian and Baltic publishers came on board, and then in 2015 the French company Libellud acquired the French and English rights—and by the end of the year, Mysterium was everywhere. That's because Libellud is in partnership with Asmodee.

Asmodee is a comparative newcomer to the game scene; set up in 1995 in France, to publish and distribute games to the hobby market. Although it did well through the boom years of the collectible card game (CCG) craze, it remained a modest size until 2007, when it began to buy up small publishers with interesting games. In 2013, it was bought by a private equity firm, Eurazeo, for $184 million (€143 million, £121 million), and built a portfolio by acquiring the rights to many of the modern classics that were driving the board-game renaissance. By 2018, Asmodee controlled the rights to many bestsellers, Spiel des Jahres winners, and gateway games like Settlers of Catan (now just called Catan), Carcassonne, Ticket to Ride, Pandemic, Pandemic Legacy, Spot It! (Dobble in the UK), Splendor, Sherlock Holmes Consulting Detective, 7 Wonders, and Cash 'n' Guns. Asmodee also acquired the companies Days of Wonder, Fantasy Flight, Z-Man, Plaid Hat, Space Cowboys, and smaller game publishers all over the world. They also bought game distributors, giving them more control over the way their games are supplied and sold.

In July 2018, Eurazeo sold Asmodee to another French private equity company, PAI Partners, for $1.4 billion (€1.2 billion, £1 billion). In other words, it had increased its worth by 840% in five years. Asmodee is the dominant force in the global hobby-games market today. Hasbro continues to control the family-games market in most of the world, but otherwise almost all the big names are under one French umbrella.

Opinions differ on whether this is a good or a bad thing, but the company seems to be building a solid structure for expanding the market for the best games of the last few decades. Asmodee wants games to be big. And so do we.

Above: Antoine Bauza's 7 Wonders won Spiel des Jahres' first "Kennerspiel des Jahres" (Connoisseur of the Year) award in 2011.

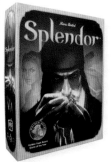

Marc André's Splendor

The Play's the Thing

Despite the rise of digital entertainment, we're in a golden age of tabletop games. Never have there been so many games, and in such quantities. The size of the game audience is growing at unprecedented speed.

According to market analysts the NPD Group, the global market for physical games grew by 12 percent in 2018—not many global markets are expanding that quickly. Also in 2018, a four-day board-game show called the International Spieltage (SPIEL) opened in Essen and attracted 190,000 visitors—that's more than went to San Diego Comic-Con the same year. Almost every city in the world now boasts at least one hobby-games shop and a games café, sometimes several. There are newsstand magazines on the subject and endless, endless websites. Board games are booming and show no signs of slowing down.

Kick-starting an explosion of games

Tabletop games is the collective term for board games, card games, miniatures, and role-playing games, and there's never been a better time to produce them. The larger companies do their manufacturing in China, but there are smaller, specialty game printers to be found all over the world. And in the last few years, the first print-on-demand producers have appeared. Now companies can take digital files for printing cards, boards, and rule books, and 3-D files for printing miniatures, and turn them into an affordable finished game. It wasn't long ago that companies had to print thousands of copies of a game to bring the manufacturing cost for each

Main image: Exploding Kittens' Tacocat card (one of many cat cards that can be used in combinations together) and Defuse card. The game-changing card game raised mroe than $8.8 million (£6.7 million) from 219,382 backers on crowd-funding platform, Kickstarter.

EXPLODING KITTENS • Year/period created: *2015* • Designer: *Matthew Inman, Elan Lee, and Shane Small* • Place of origin: *US* • Number of players: *2–5* • Time to play: *15 minutes* • Complexity: *Medium*

unit down to a profitable level, but these days that number can be as low as 10 copies.

And then there's Kickstarter. Set up in Brooklyn, New York, in 2009, it was one of the first online crowdfunding platforms. Anyone can list a dream project, create a page describing their idea, and ask for pledges against a target figure. If donations pass the target, then the project is funded, and once the project is made, all the backers receive what they pledged. It's an internet-age reinvention of the 18th-century publishing model of subscriptions, which paid for the creation of Samuel Johnson's dictionary among many others things.

Kickstarter has had an extraordinary effect on the way games are produced and sold. In 2018, a total of 2,337 tabletop games were successfully launched through the site, raising more than $165 million, up 20 percent on the year before. That's an average of $70,603 per game—though with titles like Tainted Grail: The Fall of Avalon raising more than $6.25 million on its own, most titles raise a good deal less. Not every project is going to make its creators rich, but these days, with digital printing and global shipping, it's never been easier to get your game made and shipped to an eager audience.

Games are Kickstarter's biggest sector, and board games dwarf video games, both for the number of projects and the amount of money raised.

Indie game developer Luke Crane runs the game section of Kickstarter. He has crowdfunded a number of his own designs, including The Burning Wheel, Torchbearer, and Mouse Guard.

Three of the top-ten most-funded Kickstarter projects ever are board games: The 7th Continent ($7,072,757), Exploding Kittens ($8,782,571), and Kingdom Death: Monster 1.5 (a jaw-dropping $12,393,139).

Above: Selection of cards from Exploding Kittens: The Exploding Kitten card means it's game over for whoever draws it, unless they have a Defuse card. The Nope card cancels some actions.

Only 352 video games were funded successfully in 2018, making a total of $41.5 million.

Feisty independent games such as Exploding Kittens, Cards Against Humanity, and Gloomhaven all began life on Kickstarter. Exploding Kittens is a card-draw game described as "kitty-powered Russian Roulette." Whoever draws the Exploding Kitten card explodes and is out of the game—unless they're able to avoid that fate, which is what makes the game so strategic.

Kickstarter enables designers to get their ideas validated without having to print thousands of copies first. It also means that they can sell directly to the public and enjoy receiving the revenue upfront. It's no surprise that some game companies now kick-start everything they publish. Some don't bother dealing with distributors or stores at all. Kickstarter has also proved to be a fertile platform for pushing game designs as far as they can go. The massive $140 box of Gloomhaven probably wouldn't have succeeded if it had launched through shops, but its two Kickstarters raised more than $4 million and a flood of publicity. With this, the designer and publisher Isaac Childres was able to persuade retailers there was enough demand that they should stock it.

Above: Base and stacking piece from Beasts of Balance, which communicate to the iPad that recreates the scene in the virtual world.

Beasts of Balance battle cards

Blending physical and digital games

The app-enabled stacking game Beasts of Balance raised a comparatively modest £168,000 ($227,000) on its first Kickstarter try, but this did enable the game to be manufactured. Then the publishers, Sensible Object, were able to show off how good it looked to retailers and find new sales avenues—including Apple stores. An unusual home for board games, Apple was prepared to sell Beasts of Balance alongside iPads and iPhones partly because of its high-class look and because it crosses the divide between physical and digital games, using phones and tablets as part of the experience.

There have been digital versions of physical games like Chess ever since Alan Turing created Turochamp in the early 1950s. Crossover games

BEASTS OF BALANCE • Year/period created: **2016** • Designer: **George Buckenham and Alex Fleetwood (Sensible Object)** • Place of origin: **UK** • Number of players: **1–5** • Time to play: **15–30 minutes** • Complexity: **Medium**

appeared with early home computers, for example, MB's Dark Tower from 1981 was a fantasy quest game with a looming tower in the middle of a board that contained a small dedicated computer to track rations, work out the battles, play music, and more. In 1993, Parker Brothers released Legend of Zagor designed by Ian Livingstone and based on the Fighting Fantasy gamebook of the same name. It was a fun dungeon-crawling game with superb plastic miniatures and an electronic voice that relayed events to players.

Tabletop games that use apps or software instead of a referee or an adversary arrived in 2007 with The Eye of Judgment for the PlayStation 3. This was a collectible card game with proper cards that had machine-readable codes printed on each one, which the PlayStation Eye camera could identify—so you played the game in the real world, with the battle appearing in 3-D glory on the screen.

Beasts of Balance takes the blend of physical/digital further. It's a physical stacking game like Jenga, but every piece is different, and each one contains an RFID chip. The base contains an RFID reader, so it knows which piece has been played, and also a digital scale so it knows whether the piece has been successfully added to the precarious stack. If it has, the base sends a signal to the tablet or phone, and that piece appears on the screen. If pieces fall off, the base senses that, too, and gives you a volcanic time limit to restack them or it's game over.

Beasts of Balance is a cooperative game about working together with other people to create a balanced ecosystem—balanced in the real world as well as in the digital world. As new creatures appear on the screen, they may take up new spaces or interbreed to create hybrids like the *sheagle*—a shark-eagle cross—which occupies a particular environment in the game. You don't compete against the other players, but rather against your own earlier scores—or just for the pleasure of play.

The company Sensible Object is at the forefront of these physical/ digital games that draw on the strengths from each side to create something that simply wasn't possible five years ago. Their second game, When in Rome, is a travel trivia board game

Beasts of Balance box

Beasts of Balance's eponymous beasts resemble a bear, eagle, shark, warthog, toucan and octopus. "Nurturing" and "enhancing" blocks resemble the elements earth, air, water and fire. Mythical creatures, including a dragon, have also been added.

RFID (radio-frequency identification) enables physical objects to communicate with computers. It's used in many industries, but has brought a new level of functionality to games.

Above: Amazon's Alexa, the star piece in When in Rome, with the physical board, cards, and miniatures.

There are many games you can play with Amazon's interactive assistant, Alexa, including classics like Bingo and Tic-Tac-Toe. And if you're ever short of dice, Alexa can call random numbers for you.

released in 2018 for Amazon's Alexa, the voice-responsive home speaker. When in Rome has a physical board and pieces, but it's the digital device that asks the questions and can understand the answers.

Travel trivia games have a checkered history. Ubi, the second game by the creators of Trivial Pursuit, was about world knowledge. It was released in 1986 and bombed into such deep obscurity that it doesn't even have a Wikipedia page. When in Rome has taken steps to avoid that fate: it's lighter, more humorous, and more of a social game than a test of knowledge.

New ways to play

As well as the field of physical/digital crossovers, some physical games have gone completely digital. Asmodée has an entire department creating app versions of its successful board games; Ignacy Trzewiczek's Detective has an online database that you use to help solve the cases; and there are stand-alone programs like Tabletop Simulator that let gamers play a huge range of board games over the internet, against opponents around the world, with such realism that you can even flip the virtual table in disgust if things are going badly. There are advantages to playing this way beyond just the computer shuffling the cards and doing the scoring. You can play asynchronously: the app alerts you when your opponent has played and it's your turn. This means you don't have to sit around and wait while your opponent decides their move. Instead, you can play games that stretch over days or weeks, and you can play several at the same time. This echoes how people played Chess and Diplomacy by mail in the old days. Just like in game design, there are few new ideas in games, but there are new ways of using old ones.

WHEN IN ROME • Year/period created: **2018** • Designer: **George Buckenham and Alex Fleetwood (Sensible Object)** • Place of origin: **UK** Number of players: **2–8** • Time to play: **30 minutes–2 hours** • Complexity: **Medium**

THE MIND • Year/period created: **2018** • Designer: **Wolfgang Warsch** • Place of origin: **Germany**
Number of players: **2–4** • Time to play: **15 minutes** • Complexity: **Low**

As digital technology evolves, there will still be a huge audience for the classics: they are a *lingua franca* that lets you play Chess or Go or Mancala against people in Africa or Japan or India, because the shared knowledge of the game is your language. And the part of our brain that responds to play will always demand that we find a place to sit down with some friends, some cards, some dice or counters and spend time in the special space that Johan Huizinga called "the magic circle" (see p.118), where real life is suspended for an escapist world of game play.

Minds of the future

As game designers, we're asked from time to time if there really are still new board games to be invented. Surely, after 8,000 years, haven't humans tried everything that can be done with dice and cards? But the mind of a game designer is an extraordinary thing. Just take Wolfgang Warsch and his 2018 game The Mind, short-listed for the Spiel des Jahres. It's an idea so simple that you'd think someone must have invented it before. But no, this is new, unlike anything else, and it takes less than a paragraph to explain.

In 2012, actor and gamer Wil Wheaton launched Tabletop, a web-only video series of him playing modern board games with friends. The first episode got more than three million views on YouTube.

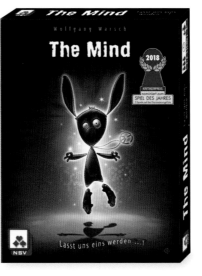

Right: Selection of cards and packaging from The Mind. Each deck has 100 cards numbered 1–100, three star cards and five life point cards (both of which are life lines), and 12 level cards.

Level 4

Sub-kognitive
Wahrnehmung

YouTube channels
and video blogs
like The Dice Tower
and Shut Up &
Sit Down can help
players choose
from the myriad
of games coming
to market.

The Mind is a co-op game played with a deck of cards, numbered from 1–100. Every player gets a hand (in round one it's one card, in round two it's two, and so on), and as a group you have to play them face up in order, lowest to highest, without talking to each other. That's it. That's the whole game. It sounds like nothing, like anyone could have come up with it.

And yet it's one of the most mind-twisting, engrossing experiences of the last few years. Someone plays the 13 card, and your lowest is 32. Surely someone else has to have a card lower than that, but nobody's making a move. Should you play? How long do you wait to see if anyone else goes? How much tension can you bear before you make the jump? A session of The Mind has more long, significant pauses than a Samuel Beckett play. Playing a card correctly feels like a victory, completing a round is a triumph, and finishing the whole game—well, we haven't managed it yet. But when the cards come right and, as a team, you bang down three or four cards in perfect synchronization, it feels like the purest magic.

Games are magic, and part of that magic is that anyone can make them. You don't need a qualification; all you need is an idea. Pick up some pebbles or draw a few lines in the dirt, and see what happens when you try moving them in different ways. If one rule's not working, take it out and try something else. Maybe bring in an idea from another game and see if it fits. Be prepared for the first few versions to be rough, but pretty soon you'll start to see which bits are working well, and you can steer the design in that direction. Keep at it, testing and revising, and find some friends to try it with.

There are 100 games called out in this book, milestones where the course of gaming history took a new move toward the present. But what of the future? Will there be a new twist on a classic on the shelves offering a different way of playing? The search is never ending.

We've had our go— now it's your turn.

Spiel des Jahres Winners

1979	**Hare and Tortoise**	David Parlett
1980	**Rummikub**	Ephraim Hertzano
1981	**Focus**	Sid Sackson
1982	**Enchanted Forest**	Alex Randolph, Michel Matschoss
1983	**Scotland Yard**	Werner Schlegel, Dorothy Garrels, Fritz Ifland, Manfred Burggraf, Werner Scheerer, Wolf Hoermann
1984	**Railway Rivals**	David Watts
1985	**Sherlock Holmes: Consulting Detective**	Raymond Edwards, Suzanne Goldberg, Gary Grady
1986	**Top Secret Spies**	Wolfgang Kramer
1987	**Auf Achse**	Wolfgang Kramer
1988	**Barbarossa**	Klaus Teuber
1989	**Café International**	Rudi Hoffmann
1990	**Adel Verpflichtet**	Klaus Teuber
1991	**Drunter und Drüber**	Klaus Teuber
1992	**Um Reifenbreite**	Rob Bontenbal
1993	**Call my Bluff**	Richard Borg
1994	**Manhattan**	Andreas Seyfarth
1995	**The Settlers of Catan**	Klaus Teuber
1996	**El Grande**	Wolfgang Kramer and Richard Ulrich
1997	**Mississippi Queen**	Werner Hodel
1998	**Elfenland**	Alan R. Moon
1999	**Tikal**	Wolfgang Kramer and Michael Kiesling
2000	**Torres**	Wolfgang Kramer and Michael Kiesling
2001	**Carcassonne**	Klaus-Jürgen Wrede
2002	**Villa Paletti**	Bill Payne
2003	**Alhambra**	Dirk Henn
2004	**Ticket to Ride**	Alan R. Moon

2001 winner Carcassonne

INDEX

BIBLIOGRAPHY

Books
Ancient Board Games in Perspective: Papers from the 1990 British Museum colloquium with additional contributions ed. I. L. Finkel (British Museum, 2008);
A History of Board Games Other Than Chess by H. J. R. Murrah (Gardners Books, 1952);
Board And Table Games from Many Civilizations by R. C. Bell (Dover edition, 1979);
Oxford History of Board Games by David Parlett (OUP, 1999), rereleased as *Parlett's History of Board Games* (Echo Point Books & Media, 2018);
The Oxford Guide to Card Games by David Parlett (OUP, 1990);
Playing at the World by Jon Peterson (Unreason Press, 2012);
Zones of Control, ed. Pat Harrigan and Matthew G. Kirschenbaum (MIT Press, 2016);
It's All A Game by Tristram Donovan (Atlantic Books, 2018);
Floor Games and Little Wars by H. G. Wells (Frank Palmer, 1911 and 1913), reprinted as one volume (Dover Publications, 2015);
Table Games of Georgian and Victorian Days by F. R. B. Whitehouse (Priory Press, 1971);
Storytelling in the Modern Board Game by Marco Arnaudo (McFarland, 2018);
Play the Game ed. Brian Love (Michael Joseph, 1978);
Six Victorian & Edwardian Board Games by Olivia Bristol (Michael O'Mara Books, 1995);
Games of the World ed. Frederic V. Grunfeld (Ballantine Books, 1975);
The New Games Treasury by Merilyn Simonds Mohr (Houghton Mifflin, 1997);
The Family Book of Games by David Pritchard (Michael Joseph, 1983);
Homo Ludens by Johan Huizinga (1938);
Man, Play and Games by Roger Caillois (reprinted by University of Illinois Press, 2001);
Georgian and Victorian Board Games: the Liman Collection ed. Ellen Liman (Pointed Leaf Press, 2017);
Hobby Games: The 100 Best by James Lowder (Green Ronin Publishing, 2017).

Useful websites
www.boardgamegeek.com
www.metmuseum.org
www.britishmuseum.org
https://collections.vam.ac.uk
www.tabletopgaming.co.uk
"Geographical board game: promoting tourism and travel in Georgian England and Wales" www.tandfonline.com (11 Feb. 2016);
"The New Game of Human Life, 1790" by Christopher Rovee. BRANCH: Britain, Representation and Nineteenth-Century History. Ed. Dino Franco Felluga. Extension of Romanticism and Victorianism www.branchcollective.org (published March 2015);
"Rithmomachia, the Philosophers' Game: A Mediaeval Battle of Numbers" by Peter Mebben http://jducoeur.org/game-hist/mebben.rith.html;
"Soviet board games" by Oleg Tarasov (14 Jan. 2011) https://statehistory.ru/1365/Sovetskie-nastolnye-igry/;
"Die Kenntnis des Dominospiels in Europa: Archäologie, Geschichte, Bibliographie", *Board Game Studies Journal*, by I. Braun (2016) https://doi.org/10.1515/bgs-2016-0004;
Conference Papers, Seminars & Specialist Presentations by Jill Shefrin, http://teetotum.ca

IMAGE CREDITS

DK | Penguin Random House

Senior Editor Emma Grange
Project Art Editor Jon Hall
Picture Research Sumedha Chopra and Martin Copeland
Senior Pre-production Producer Jennifer Murray
Senior Producer Mary Slater
Managing Editor Sadie Smith
Managing Art Editor Vicky Short
Publisher Julie Ferris
Art Director Lisa Lanzarini
Publishing Director Simon Beecroft

Cover design by LLÖ

Ian Livingstone's dedication:
To Steve, Mark, Skye, Peter, and Clive of the Games Night Club

James Wallis's dedication:
To Cat, Eliza, and Flossie, the best playtesters in the world

DK would like to thank: Ian Livingstone and James Wallis for their text and expertise;
Holly Nielsen for historical consultancy work on chapters 7, 8, 10, 11, and 12; Jess Tapolcai
and LLÖ for design; Jennette ElNaggar, Rosie Peet, and Nicole Reynolds for editorial
help; Gary Ombler for photography; and Vanessa Bird for the index.

First American Edition, 2019
Published in the United States by DK Publishing
1450 Broadway, Suite 801, New York, NY 10018

Text copyright © Ian Livingstone, 2019

A catalog record for this book is available from the Library of Congress.
ISBN 978-1-4654-8575-5

DK books are available at special discounts when purchased in bulk for sales
promotions, premiums, fund-raising, or educational use. For details, contact:
DK Publishing Special Markets, 1450 Broadway, Suite 801, New York, NY 10018
SpecialSales@dk.com

Printed and bound in China

A WORLD OF IDEAS:
SEE ALL THERE IS TO KNOW

www.dk.com